PENGUIN

Fr

GW00632158

1. *Voices of Akenfield* Ronald Blythe
2. *The Wood* John Stewart Collis
3. *From Dover to the Wen* William Cobbett
4. *The Pleasures of English Food* Alan Davidson
5. *Through England on a Side-Saddle* Celia Fiennes
6. *Elegy Written in a Country Churchyard and Other Poems* Various
7. *A Shropshire Lad* A. E. Housman
8. *Cathedrals and Castles* Henry James
9. *Walks in the Wheat-fields* Richard Jefferies
10. *The Beauties of a Cottage Garden* Gertrude Jekyll
11. *Country Churches* Simon Jenkins
12. *A Wiltshire Diary* Francis Kilvert
13. *Some Country Houses and their Owners* James Lees-Milne
14. *The Clouded Mirror* L. T. C. Rolt
15. *Let Us Now Praise Famous Gardens* Vita Sackville-West
16. *One Green Field* Edward Thomas
17. *English Folk Songs* Ralph Vaughan Williams and A. L. Lloyd
18. *Country Lore and Legends* Jennifer Westwood and Jacqueline Simpson
19. *Birds of Selborne* Gilbert White
20. *Life at Grasmere* Dorothy and William Wordsworth

FROM DOVER TO THE WEN

William Cobbett

English Penguin *Journeys*

PENGUIN BOOKS

Published by the Penguin Group
Penguin Books Ltd, 80 Strand, London WC2R 0RL, England
Penguin Group (USA) Inc., 375 Hudson Street, New York, New York 10014, USA
Penguin Group (Canada), 90 Eglinton Avenue East, Suite 700, Toronto, Ontario, Canada M4P 2Y3
(a division of Pearson Penguin Canada Inc.)
Penguin Ireland, 25 St Stephen's Green, Dublin 2, Ireland
(a division of Penguin Books Ltd)
Penguin Group (Australia), 250 Camberwell Road, Camberwell, Victoria 3124, Australia
(a division of Pearson Australia Group Pty Ltd)
Penguin Books India Pvt Ltd, 11 Community Centre, Panchsheel Park, New Delhi – 110 017, India
Penguin Group (NZ), 67 Apollo Drive, Rosedale, North Shore 0632, New Zealand
(a division of Pearson New Zealand Ltd)
Penguin Books (South Africa) (Pty) Ltd, 24 Sturdee Avenue, Rosebank, Johannesburg 2196, South Africa

Penguin Books Ltd, Registered Offices: 80 Strand, London WC2R 0RL, England

www.penguin.com

These extracts taken from *Rural Rides*, first published 1830
Published in Penguin Books 2009

3

All rights reserved

Set by Rowland Phototypesetting Ltd, Bury St Edmunds, Suffolk
Printed in England by Clays Ltd, St Ives plc

ISBN: 978-0-141-19055-6

www.greenpenguin.co.uk

A Note on the Text

'From Dover to the Wen' is taken from *Rural Rides* (first published 1830)

Contents

From Dover, through the Isle of Thanet, by
Canterbury and Faversham, across to
Maidstone, up to Tonbridge, through the
Weald of Kent and over the hills by
Westerham and Hays, to the Wen   1

From Kensington, Across Surrey, and Along
that County   41

From Chilworth, in Surrey, to Winchester   60

From Winchester to Burghclere   81

From Dover, through the Isle of Thanet, by Canterbury and Faversham, across to Maidstone, up to Tonbridge, through the Weald of Kent and over the hills by Westerham and Hays, to the Wen

Dover,
Wednesday, Sept. 3. 1823 Evening

On Monday I was balancing in my own mind whether I should go to France or not. To-day I have decided the question in the negative, and shall set off this evening for the Isle of Thanet; that spot so famous for corn.

[. . .] In describing the parts of the country over which I have travelled I have often mentioned the *chalk-ridge* and also the *sand-ridge*, which I had traced, running parallel with each other from about Farnham, in Surrey, to Sevenoaks, in Kent. [. . .] In going up from Chilworth and Albury, through Dorking, Reigate, Godstone, and so on, the two chains, or ridges, approach so near to each other, that, in many places, you actually have a chalk-bank to your right and a sand-bank to your left, at not more than forty yards from each other. In some places, these chains of hills run off from each other to a great distance, even to a distance of twenty miles. They then approach again towards each other, and so they go on. I was always desirous to ascertain whether these chains, or ridges, continued on thus *to the sea*. I have now found that they do. And, if you go out into the channel, at Folkestone, there you see a sand-cliff and a chalk-cliff. Folkestone stands upon the sand, in a little dell about seven hundred or eight hundred yards from the very termination of the ridge. All the way along, the chalk-ridge is the most lofty, until you come to Leith Hill and Hindhead; and here, at Folkestone, the sand-ridge tapers off in a sort of flat towards the sea. The land is like what it is at Reigate, a very steep hill; a hill of full a mile high, and bending exactly in the same manner as the hill at Reigate does. The turnpike-road winds up it and goes over it in exactly the same manner as that at Reigate. The land to the south of the hill begins a poor, thin, white loam upon the chalk; soon gets to be a very fine, rich loam upon the chalk; goes on till it mingles the chalky loam with the sandy loam; and thus it goes on down to the sea-beach, or to the edge of the cliff. It is a beautiful bed of earth here, resembling in extent that on the south side of Portsdown Hill rather than that of Reigate. The crops here are always good if they are good any where. A large part of this fine tract of land, as well as the little town of Sandgate (which is a beautiful little place upon the beach itself), and also great part of the town of Folkestone belong, they tell me, to Lord Radnor, who takes his title of Viscount, from Folkestone. Upon the hill, begins, and continues on for some miles, that stiff red loam, approaching to a clay, which I have several times described as forming the soil at the top of this chalk-ridge. I spoke of it in the Register of the 16th of August last, page 409, and I then said, that it was like the land on the top of this very ridge at Ashmansworth in the North of Hampshire. At Reigate, you find precisely the same soil upon the top of the hill, a very red, clayey sort of loam, with big yellow flint stones in it. Every where, the soil is the same upon the top of the high part of this ridge. I have now found it to be the same, on the edge of the sea, that I found it on the North East corner of Hampshire.

From the hill, you keep descending all the way to Dover, a distance of about six miles, and it is absolutely six miles of down hill. On your right, you have the lofty land which forms a series of chalk cliffs, from the top of which you look into the sea: on your left, you have ground that goes rising up from you in the same sort of way. The turnpike-road goes down the middle of a valley, each side of which, as far as you can see, may be about a mile and a half. It is six miles long, you will remember; and here, therefore, with very little interruption, very few chasms, there are *eighteen square miles of corn*. It is a patch such as you very seldom see, and especially of corn so good as it is here. I should think that the wheat all along here would average pretty nearly four quarters to the acre. A few oats are sown. A great deal of barley, and that a very fine crop.

The town of Dover is like other sea-port towns; but really, much more clean, and with less blackguard people in it than I ever observed in any sea-port before. It is a most picturesque place, to be sure. On one side of it rises, upon the top of a very steep hill, the Old Castle, with all its fortifications. On the other side of it there is another chalk-hill, the side of which is pretty nearly perpendicular, and rises up from sixty to an hundred feet higher than the tops of the houses, which stand pretty nearly close to the foot of the hill.

I got into Dover rather late. It was dusk when I was going down the street towards the quay. I happened to look up, and was quite astonished to perceive cows grazing upon a spot apparently fifty feet above the tops of the houses, and measuring horizontally not, perhaps, more than ten or twenty feet from a line which would have formed a continuation into the air. I went up to the same spot, the next day, myself; and you actually look down upon the houses, as you look out of a window, upon people in the street. The valley that runs down from Folkestone is, when it gets to Dover, crossed by another valley that runs down from Canterbury, or, at least, from the Canterbury direction. It is in the gorge of this cross valley that Dover is built. The two chalk-hills jut out into the sea, and the water that comes up between them forms a harbour for this ancient, most interesting, and beautiful place. On the hill to the North, stands the Castle of Dover, which is fortified in the ancient manner, except on the sea-side, where it has the steep *cliff* for a fortification. On the South side of the town, the hill is, I believe, rather more lofty than that on the North side; and here is that cliff which is described by SHAKSPEARE in the Play of King Lear. It is fearfully steep, certainly. Very nearly perpendicular for a considerable distance. The grass grows well, to the very tip of the cliff; and you see cows and sheep grazing there with as much unconcern as if grazing in the bottom of a valley. It was not, however, these natural curiosities that took me over *this* hill, I went to see, with my own eyes, something of the sorts of means that had been made use of to squander away countless millions of money. Here is a hill containing probably a couple of square miles or more, hollowed like a honey-comb. Here are line upon line, trench upon trench, cavern upon cavern, bomb-proof upon bomb-proof; in short the very sight of the thing convinces you that either madness the most humiliating, or profligacy the most scandalous must have been at work here for years. The question that every man of sense asks, is: What reason had you to suppose that the *French would ever come to this hill* to attack it, while the rest of the country was so much more easy to assail? However, let any man of good plain understanding, go and look at the works that have here been performed, and that are now all tumbling into ruin. Let him ask what this cavern was for; what that ditch was for; what this tank was for; and why all these horrible holes and hiding-places at an expense of millions upon millions? Let this scene be brought and placed under the eyes of the people of England, and let them be told that Pitt and Dundas and Perceval had these things done to prevent the country from being conquered; with voice unanimous the nation would instantly exclaim: Let the French or let the devil take us, rather than let us resort to means of defence like these. This is, perhaps, the only set of fortifications in the world ever framed for mere *hiding*. There is no appearance of any intention to annoy an enemy. It is a parcel of holes made in a hill, to hide Englishmen from Frenchmen. Just as if the Frenchmen would come to this hill! Just as if they would not go (if they came at all) and land in Romney Marsh, or on Pevensey Level, or any where else, rather than come to this hill; rather than come to crawl up SHAKSPEARE's cliff. All the way along the coast, from this very hill to Portsmouth; or pretty nearly all the way, is a flat. What the devil should they come to this hill for, then? And, when you ask this question, they tell you that it is to have an army here *behind* the French, after they had marched into the country! And for a purpose like this; for a purpose so stupid, so senseless, so mad as this, and withal, so scandalously disgraceful, more brick and stone have been buried in this hill than would go to build a neat new cottage for every labouring man in the counties of Kent and of Sussex! Dreadful is the scourge of such Ministers. However, those who supported them will now have to suffer. The money must have been squandered purposely, and for the worst ends. Fool as Pitt was; unfit as an old hack of a lawyer, like Dundas, was to judge of the means of defending the country, stupid as both these fellows were, and as their brother lawyer, Perceval, was too: unfit as these lawyers were to judge in any such a case, they must have known that this was an useless expenditure of money. They must have known that; and, therefore, their general folly; their general ignorance is no apology for their conduct. What they wanted, was to prevent the landing, not of Frenchmen, but of French principles; that is to say, to prevent the example of the French from being alluring to the people of England. The devil a bit did they care for the Bourbons. They rejoiced at the killing of the King. They rejoiced at the atheistical decree. They rejoiced at every thing calculated to alarm the timid and to excite horror in the people of

England in general. They wanted to keep out of England those principles which had a natural tendency to destroy borough-mongering, and to put an end to peculation and plunder. No matter whether by the means of Martello Towers, making a great chalk-hill a honey-comb, cutting a canal thirty feet wide to stop the march of the armies of the Danube and the Rhine; no matter how they squandered the money, so that it silenced some and made others bawl to answer their great purpose of preventing French example from having an influence in England. Simply their object was this: to make the French people miserable; to force back the Bourbons upon them as a *means* of making them miserable; to degrade France, to make the people wretched; and then to have to say to the people of England, Look there: *see what they have got by their attempts to obtain liberty!* This was their object. They did not want Martello Towers and honey-combed chalk-hills, and mad canals: they did not want these to keep out the French armies. The borough-mongers and the parsons cared nothing about the French armies. It was the French example that the lawyers, borough-mongers and parsons wished to keep out. And what have they done? It is impossible to be upon this honey-combed hill; upon this enormous mass of anti-jacobin expenditure, without seeing the chalk-cliffs of Calais and the corn-fields of France. At this season, it is impossible to see those fields without knowing that the farmers are getting in their corn there as well as here; and it is impossible to think of that fact without reflecting at the same time, on the example which the farmers of France hold out to the farmers of England. Looking down from this very anti-jacobin hill, this day, I saw the parsons' shocks of wheat and barley, left in the field after the farmer had taken his away. Turning my head, and looking across the Channel, 'There,' said I, pointing to France, 'there the spirited and sensible people have ridded themselves of this burden, of which our farmers so bitterly complain.' It is impossible not to recollect here, that, in numerous petitions, sent up, too, by the *loyal*, complaints have been made that the English farmer has to carry on a competition against the French farmer who has *no tithes to pay!* Well, *loyal gentlemen*, why do not you petition, then, to be relieved from tithes? What do you mean else? Do you mean to call upon our big gentlemen at Whitehall for them to compel the French to pay tithes? Oh, you loyal fools! Better hold your tongues about the French not paying tithes. Better do that, at any rate; for never will they pay tithes again.

Here is a large tract of *land* upon these hills at Dover, which is the property of the public, having been purchased at an enormous expense. This is now let out as pasture land to people of the town. I dare say that the *letting of this land is a curious affair*. If there were a Member for Dover who would do what he ought to do, he would soon get before the public a list of the tenants, and of the rents paid by them. I should like very much to see such list. Butterworth, the bookseller in Fleet Street; he who is a sort of metropolitan of the methodists, is one of the Members for Dover. The other is, I believe, that Wilbraham or Bootle or Bostle Wilbraham, or some such name, that is a Lancashire magistrate. So that Dover is prettily set up. However, there is nothing of this sort that can, in the present state of things be deemed to be of any real consequence. As long as the people at White-hall can go on paying the interest of the debt in full, so long will there be no change worth the attention of any rational man. In the meanwhile, the French nation will be going on rising over us; and our Ministers will be cringing and crawling to every nation upon earth who is known to possess a cannon or a barrel of powder.

This very day I have read Mr CANNING's Speech at Liverpool, with a Yankee Consul sitting on his right hand. Not a word now about the bits of bunting and the fir frigates, but now, America is the lovely daughter, who, in a moment of excessive love, has gone off with a lover (to wit, the French) and left the tender mother to mourn! What a fop! And this is the man that talked so big and so bold. This is the clever, the profound, the blustering, too, and, above all things, *'the high-spirited'* Mr CANNING. However, more of this, hereafter. I must get from this Dover, as fast as I can.

Sandwich,
Wednesday, 3 Sept. Night

I got to this place about half an hour after the ringing of the eight o'clock bell, or Curfew, which I heard at about two miles distance from the place. From the town of Dover you come up the Castle-Hill, and have a most beautiful view from the top of it. You have the sea, the chalk cliffs of Calais, the high land at Boulogne, the town of Dover just under you, the valley towards Folkestone, and the much more beautiful valley towards Canterbury;

and, going on a little further, you have the Downs and the Essex or Suffolk coast in full view, with a most beautiful corn country to ride along through. The corn was chiefly cut between Dover and Walmer. The barley almost all cut and tied up in sheaf. Nothing but the beans seemed to remain standing along here. They are not quite so good as the rest of the corn; but they are by no means bad. When I came to the village of Walmer, I enquired for the Castle; that famous place, where PITT, DUNDAS, PERCEVAL and all the whole tribe of plotters against the French Revolution had carried on their plots. After coming through the village of Walmer, you see the entrance of the Castle away to the right. It is situated pretty nearly on the water's edge, and at the bottom of a little dell, about a furlong or so from the turnpike-road. This is now the habitation of our Great Minister, ROBERT BANKES JENKINSON, SON of CHARLES of that name. When I was told, by a girl who was leasing in a field by the road side, that that was Walmer Castle, I stopped short, pulled my horse round, looked steadfastly at the gateway, and could not help exclaiming: 'Oh, thou who inhabitest that famous dwelling; thou, who hast always been in place, let who might be out of place! Oh, thou everlasting placeman! thou sage of over-production, do but cast thine eyes upon this barley-field, where, if I am not greatly deceived, there are from *seven to eight quarters upon the acre!* Oh, thou whose Courier newspaper has just informed its readers that wheat will be seventy shillings the quarter, in the month of November: oh, thou wise man, I pray thee come forth, from thy Castle, and tell me what thou wilt do if wheat should happen to be, at the appointed time *thirty-five* shillings, instead of *seventy shillings*, the quarter. Sage of over-production, farewell. If thou hast life, thou wilt be Minister, as long as thou canst pay the interest of the Debt in full, but not one moment longer. The moment thou ceasest to be able to squeeze from the Normans a sufficiency to count down to the Jews their full tale, that moment, thou great stern-path-of-duty man, thou wilt begin to be taught the true meaning of the words *Ministerial Responsibility.'*

DEAL is a most villanous place. It is full of filthy-looking people. Great desolation of abomination has been going on here; tremendous barracks, partly pulled down and partly tumbling down, and partly occupied by soldiers. Every thing seems upon the parish. I was glad to hurry along through it, and to leave its inns and public-houses to be occupied by the tarred, and trowsered, and blue-and-buff crew whose very vicinage I always detest. From Deal you come along to Upper Deal, which it seems was the original village; thence upon a beautiful road to Sandwich, which is a rotten Borough. Rottenness, putridity is excellent for land, but bad for Boroughs. This place, which is as villanous a hole as one would wish to see, is surrounded by some of the finest land in the world. Along on one side of it, lies a marsh. On the other sides of it is land which they tell me bears *seven quarters* of wheat to an acre. It is certainly very fine; for I saw large pieces of radish-seed on the road side; this seed is grown for the seedsmen in London; and it will grow on none but rich land. All the corn is carried here except some beans and some barley.

Canterbury,
Thursday Afternoon, 4th Sept.

In quitting Sandwich, you immediately cross a river up which vessels bring coals from the sea. This marsh is about a couple of miles wide. It begins at the sea-beach, opposite the Downs, to my right hand, coming from Sandwich, and it wheels round to my left and ends at the sea-beach, opposite Margate roads. This marsh was formerly covered with the sea, very likely; and hence the land within this sort of semicircle, the name of which is Thanet, was called an *Isle*. It is, in fact, an island now, for the same reason that Portsea is an island, and that New York is an island; for there certainly is the water in this river that goes round and connects one part of the sea with the other. I had to cross this river, and to cross the marsh, before I got into the famous Isle of Thanet, which it was my intention to cross. Soon after crossing the river, I passed by a place for making salt, and could not help recollecting that there are no excisemen in these salt-making places in France, that, before the Revolution, the French were most cruelly oppressed by the duties on salt, that they had to endure, on that account, the most horrid tyranny that ever was known, except, perhaps, that practised in an *Exchequer* that shall here be nameless; that thousands and thousands of men and women were every year sent to the galleys for what was called smuggling salt; that the fathers and even the mothers were imprisoned or whipped if the children were detected in smuggling salt: I could not help reflecting, with delight, as I looked at these salt-pans in the Isle of Thanet; I could not help reflecting, that in spite of PITT, DUNDAS, PERCEVAL, and the rest of the crew, in spite of the caverns of Dover and the Martello Towers in Romney Marsh: in spite of all the spies and all the bayonets, and the six hundred millions of Debt, and the hundred and fifty millions of dead-weight, and the two hundred millions of poor-rates that are now squeezing the borough-mongers, squeezing the farmers, puzzling the fellows at Whitehall and making Mark-lane a scene of greater interest than the Chamber of the Privy Council; with delight as I jogged along under the first beams of the sun, I reflected, that, in spite of all the malignant measures that had brought so much misery upon England, the gallant French people had ridded themselves of the tyranny which sent them to the galleys for endeavouring to use without tax the salt which God sent upon their shores. Can any man tell why we should still be paying five, or six, or seven shillings a bushel for salt, instead of one? We did pay fifteen shillings a bushel, tax. And why is two shillings a bushel kept on? Because, if they were taken off, the salt tax-gathering crew must be discharged! This tax of two shillings a bushel, causes the consumer to pay five, at the least, more than he would if there were no tax at all! When, great God! when shall we be allowed to enjoy God's gifts, in freedom, as the people of France enjoy them? – On the marsh I found the same sort of sheep as on Romney Marsh; but the cattle here are chiefly Welsh; black, and called runts. They are nice hardy cattle; and, I am told, that this is the description of cattle that they fat all the way up on this north side of Kent. – When I got upon the corn land in the Isle of Thanet, I got into a garden indeed. There is hardly any fallow; comparatively few turnips. It is a country of corn. Most of the harvest is in; but there are some fields of wheat and of barley not yet housed. A great many pieces of lucerne, and all of them very fine. I left Ramsgate to my right about three miles, and went right across the island to Margate; but that place is so thickly settled with stock-jobbing cuckolds, at this time of the year, that, having no fancy to get their horns stuck into me, I turned away to my left when I got within about half a mile of the town. I got to a little hamlet, where I breakfasted; but could get no corn for my horse, and no bacon for myself! All was corn around me. Barns, I should think, two hundred feet long; ricks of enormous size and most numerous; crops of wheat, five quarters to an acre, on the average; and a public-house without either bacon or corn! The labourers' houses, all along through this island, beggarly in the extreme. The people dirty, poor-looking; ragged, but particularly *dirty*. The men and boys with dirty faces, and dirty smock-frocks, and dirty shirts; and, good God! what a difference between the wife of a labouring man here, and the wife of a labouring man in the forests and woodlands of Hampshire and Sussex! Invariably have I observed, that the richer the soil, and the more destitute of woods; that is to say, the more purely a corn country, the more miserable the labourers. The cause is this, the great, the big bull frog grasps all. In this beautiful island every inch of land is appropriated by the rich. No hedges, no ditches, no commons, no grassy lanes: a country divided into great farms; a few trees surround the great farm-house.

All the rest is bare of trees; and the wretched labourer has not a stick of wood, and has no place for a pig or cow to graze, or even to lie down upon. The rabbit countries are the countries for labouring men. There the ground is not so valuable. There it is not so easily appropriated by the few. Here, in this island, the work is almost all done by the horses. The horses plough the ground; they sow the ground; they hoe the ground; they carry the corn home; they thresh it out; and they carry it to market: nay, in this island, they *rake* the ground; they rake up the straggling straws and ears; so that they do the whole, except the reaping and the mowing. It is impossible to have an idea of any thing more miserable than the state of the labourers in this part of the country.

After coming by Margate, I passed a village called MONCKTON, and another called SARR. At SARR there is a bridge, over which you come out of the island, as you go into it over the bridge at SANDWICH. At MONCKTON they had *seventeen men working on the roads*, though the harvest was not quite in, and though, of course, it had all to be threshed out; but, at MONCKTON, they had *four threshing machines*; and they have three threshing machines at SARR, though there, also, they have several men upon the roads! This is a shocking state of things; and, in spite of every thing that the Jenkinsons and the Scots can do, this state of things must be changed.

At SARR, or a little way further back, I saw a man who had just begun to reap a field of canary seed. The plants were too far advanced to be cut in order to be bleached for the making of plat; but I got the reaper to select me a few green stalks that grew near a bush that stood on the outside of the piece. These I have brought on with me, in order to give them a trial. At SARR I began to cross the marsh, and had, after this, to come through the village of UP-STREET, and another village called STEADY, before I got to Canterbury. At Up-STREET I was struck with the words written upon a board which was fastened upon a pole, which pole was standing in a garden near a neat little box of a house. The words were these: 'PARADISE PLACE. *Spring guns and steel traps are set here.*' A pretty idea it must give us of Paradise to know that spring guns and steel traps are set in it! This is doubtless some stock-jobber's place; for, in the first place, the name is likely to have been selected by one of that crew; and, in the next place, whenever any of them go to the country, they look upon it that they are to begin a sort of warfare against every thing around them. They invariably look upon every labourer as a thief.

As you approach Canterbury, from the Isle of Thanet, you have another instance of the squanderings of the lawyer Ministers. Nothing equals the ditches, the caverns, the holes, the tanks and hiding-places of the hill at Dover; but, considerable as the City of Canterbury is, that city, within its gates, stands upon less ground than those horrible erections, the barracks of PITT, DUNDAS, and PERCEVAL. They are perfectly enormous; but thanks be unto God, they begin to crumble down. They have a sickly hue: all is lassitude about them: endless are their lawns, their gravel walks, and their ornaments; but their lawns are unshaven, their gravel walks grassy, and their ornaments putting on the garments of ugliness. You see the grass growing opposite the door-ways. A hole in the window strikes you here and there. Lamp-posts there are, but no lamps. Here are horse-barracks, foot-barracks, artillery-barracks, engineer-barracks: a whole country of barracks; but, only here and there a soldier. The thing is actually perishing. It is typical of the state of the great thing of things. It gave me inexpressible pleasure to perceive the gloom that seemed to hang over these barracks, which once swarmed with soldiers and their blithe companions, as a hive swarms with bees. These barracks now look like the environs of a hive in winter. Westminster Abbey Church is not the place for the monument of PITT, the statue of the great snorting bawler ought to be stuck up here, just in the midst of this hundred or two of acres covered with barracks. These barracks, too, were erected in order to compel the French to return to the payment of tithes; in order to bring their necks again under the yoke of the lords and the clergy. That has not been accomplished. The French, as Mr HOGGART assures us, have neither tithes, taxes, nor rates; and the people of Canterbury know that they have a *hop-duty* to pay, while Mr HOGGART, of Broad-street, tells them that he has farms to let, in France, where there are hop-gardens and where there is no hop-duty. They have lately had races at Canterbury; and the Mayor and Aldermen, in order to get the Prince Leopold to attend them, presented him with the Free-dom of the City; but it rained all the time and he did not come! The Mayor and Aldermen do not understand things half so well as this German Gentleman, who has managed his matters as well, I think, as any one that I ever heard of.

This fine old town, or, rather, city, is remarkable for cleanliness and niceness, notwithstanding it has a Cathedral in it. The country round it is very rich, and this year, while the hops are so bad in most other parts, they are not so very bad, just about Canterbury.

Elverton Farm, near Faversham,
Friday Morning, Sept. 5

In going through Canterbury, yesterday, I gave a boy sixpence to hold my horse, while I went into the Cathedral, just to thank St Swithin for the trick that he had played my friends, the Quakers. Led along by the wet weather till after the harvest had actually begun, and then to find the weather turn fine, all of a sudden! This must have soused them pretty decently; and I hear of one who, at Canterbury, has made a bargain by which he will certainly lose two thousand pounds. The land where I am now is equal to that of the Isle of Thanet. The harvest is nearly over, and all the crops have been prodigiously fine. In coming from Canterbury, you come to the top of a hill, called Baughton Hill, at four miles from Canterbury on the London road; and you there look down into one of the finest flats in England. A piece of marsh comes up nearly to FAVERSHAM; and, at the edge of that marsh lies the farm where I now am. The land here is a deep loam upon chalk; and this is also the nature of the land in the Isle of Thanet and all the way from that to Dover. The orchards grow well upon this soil. The trees grow finely, the fruit is large and of fine flavour.

In 1821 I gave Mr WM. WALLER, who lives here, some American apple-cuttings; and he has now some as fine Newtown Pippins as one would wish to see. They are very large of their sort; very free in their growth; and they promise to be very fine apples of the kind. Mr Waller had cuttings from me of several sorts, in 1822. These were cut down last year; they have, of course, made shoots this summer; and great numbers of these shoots have *fruit-spurs*, which will have blossom, if not fruit, next year. This very rarely happens, I believe; and the state of Mr WALLER's trees clearly proves to me that the introduction of these American trees would be a great improvement.

My American apples, when I left Kensington, promised to be very fine; and the apples, which I have frequently mentioned as being upon cuttings imported last Spring, promised to come to perfection; a thing which, I believe, we have not an instance of before.

Merryworth,
Friday Evening, 5th Sept.

A friend at TENTERDEN told me that, if I had a mind to know Kent, I must go through Romney Marsh to DOVER, from DOVER to SANDWICH, from Sandwich to Margate, from Margate to Canterbury, from Canterbury to Faversham, from Faversham to Maidstone, and from Maidstone to Tonbridge. I found from Mr WALLER, this morning, that the regular turnpike route, from his house to Maidstone, was through SITTINGBOURNE. I had been along that road several times; and besides, to be covered with dust was what I could not think of, when I had it in my power to get to Maidstone without it. I took the road across the country, quitting the London road, or rather, crossing it, in the dell, between OSPRINGE and GREEN-STREET. I instantly began to go up hill, slowly, indeed; but up hill. I came through the villages of NEWNHAM, DODDINGTON, RINGLESTONE, and to that of HOLLINGBOURNE. I had come up hill for *thirteen miles*, from Mr WALLER's house. At last, I got to the top of this hill, and went along, for some distance, upon level ground. I found I was got upon just the same sort of land as that on the hill at Folkestone, at Reigate, at Ropley and at Ashmansworth. The red clayey loam, mixed up with great yellow flint stones. I found *fine meadows* here, just such as are at Ashmansworth (that is to say, on the north Hampshire hills). This sort of ground is characterized by an astonishing depth that they have to go for the water. At Ashmansworth, they go to a depth of more than *three hundred feet*. As I was riding along upon the top of this hill in Kent, I saw the same beautiful sort of meadows that there are at Ashmansworth; I saw the corn backward; I was just thinking to go up to some house, to ask how far they had to go for water, when I saw a large well-bucket, and all the chains and wheels belonging to such a concern; but here was also the tackle for a *horse* to work in drawing up the water! I asked about the depth of the well; and the information I received must have been incorrect; because I was told it was three hundred yards. I asked this of a public-house keeper further on, not seeing any body where the farm-house was. I make no doubt that the depth is, as near as possible, that of Ashmansworth. Upon the top of this hill, I saw the finest field of beans that I have seen this year, and, by very far, indeed, the *finest piece of hops*. A beautiful piece of hops, surrounded by beautiful plantations of young ash, producing poles for hop-gardens. My road here pointed towards the West. It soon wheeled round towards the South; and, all of a sudden, I found myself upon the edge of a hill, as lofty and as steep as that at FOLKESTONE, at Reigate, or at ASHMANSWORTH. It was the same famous chalk-ridge that I was crossing again. When I got to the edge of the hill, and before I got off my horse to lead him down this more than mile of hill, I sat and surveyed the prospect before me, and to the right and to the left. This is what the people of Kent call the *Garden of Eden*. It is a district of meadows, corn fields, hop-gardens, and orchards of apples, pears, cherries and filberts, with very little if any land which cannot, with propriety, be called good. There are plantations of Chesnut and of Ash frequently occurring; and as these are cut when long enough to make poles for hops, they are at all times objects of great beauty.

At the foot of the hill of which I have been speaking, is the village of HOLLINGBOURNE; thence you come on to Maidstone. From MAIDSTONE to this place (MERRYWORTH) is about seven miles, and these are the finest seven miles that I have ever seen in England or any where else. The Medway is to your left, with its meadows about a mile wide. You cross the Medway, in coming out of Maidstone, and it goes and finds its way down to Rochester, through a break in the chalk-ridge. From Maidstone to Merryworth, I should think that there were hop-gardens on one half of the way on both sides of the road. Then looking across the Medway you see hop-gardens and orchards two miles deep, on the side of a gently rising ground: and this continues with you all the way from Maidstone to Merryworth. The orchards form a great feature of the country; and the plantations of Ashes and of Chesnuts that I mentioned before, add greatly to the beauty. These gardens of hops are kept very clean, in general, though some of them have been neglected this year owing to the bad appearance of the crop. The culture is sometimes mixed: that is to say, apple-trees or cherry-trees or filbert-trees and hops, in the same ground. This is a good way, they say, of raising an orchard. I do not believe it; and I think that nothing is gained by any of these mixtures. They plant apple-trees or cherry-trees in rows here; they then plant a filbert-tree close to each of these large fruit-trees; and then they cultivate the middle of the ground by planting potatoes. This is being too greedy. It is impossible that they can gain by this. What they gain one way they lose the other way; and I verily believe, that the most profitable way would be, never to mix things at all. In coming from Maidstone I passed through a village called TESTON, where LORD BASHAM has a seat.

Tonbridge,
Saturday, morning 6th Sept.

I came off from MERRYWORTH a little before five o'clock, passed the seat of LORD TORRINGTON, the friend of Mr BARRETTO. This Mr Barretto ought not to be forgotten so soon. In 1820 he sued for articles of the peace against LORD TORRINGTON, for having menaced him, in consequence of his having pressed his Lordship about some money. It seems that LORD TORRINGTON had known him in the East Indies; that they came home together, or soon after one another; that his Lordship invited Mr BARRETTO to his best parties in India; that he got him introduced at Court in England by Sidmouth; that he got him made *a fellow of the Royal Society*; and that he tried to get him introduced into Parliament. His Lordship, when BARRETTO rudely pressed him for his money, reminded him of all this, and of the many difficulties that he had had to overcome with regard to his *colour* and so forth. Nevertheless, the dingy skinned Court visitant pressed in such a way that LORD TORRINGTON was obliged to be pretty smart with him, whereupon the other sued for articles of the peace against his Lordship; but these were not granted by the Court. This Barretto issued a hand-bill at the last election as a candidate for St Albans. I am truly sorry that he was not elected. Lord Camelford threatened to put in his black fellow; but he was a sad swaggering fellow; and had, at last, too much of the borough-monger in him to do a thing so meritorious. LORD TORRINGTON's is but an indifferent looking place.

I here began to see South Down sheep again, which I had not seen since the time I left TENTERDEN. All along here the villages are at not more than two miles distance from each other. They have all large churches, and scarcely any body to go to them. At a village called HADLOW, there is a house belonging to a Mr MAY, the most singular looking thing I ever saw. An immense house stuck all over with a parcel of chimnies, or things like chimnies; little brick columns, with a sort of caps on them, looking like carnation sticks, with caps at the top to catch the earwigs. The building is all of brick, and has the oddest appearance of any thing I ever saw. This TONBRIDGE is but a common country town, though very clean, and the people looking very well. The climate must be pretty warm here; for in entering the town, I saw a large Althea Frutex in bloom, a thing rare enough, any year, and particularly a year like this.

Westerham,
Saturday, Noon, 6th Sept.

Instead of going on to the Wen along the turnpike road through SEVENOAKS, I turned to my left when I got about a mile out of TONBRIDGE, in order to come along that tract of country called the Weald of Kent; that is to say, the solid clays, which have no bottom, which are unmixed with chalk, sand, stone, or any thing else; the country of dirty roads and of oak trees. I stopped at TONBRIDGE only a few minutes; but in the Weald I stopped to breakfast at a place called Leigh. From Leigh I came to Chittingstone causeway, leaving TON-BRIDGE WELLS six miles over the hills to my left. From CHITTINGSTONE I came to BOUGH-BEACH, thence to FOUR ELMS, and thence to this little market-town of WESTERHAM which is just upon the border of Kent. Indeed, Kent, Surrey and Sussex form a joining very near to this town. Westerham, exactly like REIGATE and GODSTONE, and SEVENOAKS, and DORKING, and FOLKE-

STONE, lies between the sand-ridge and the chalk-ridge. The valley is here a little wider than at Reigate, and that is all the difference there is between the places. As soon as you get over the sand hill to the south of Reigate, you get into the Weald of Surrey; and here, as soon as you get over the sand hill to the south of Westerham, you get into the weald of Kent.

I have now, in order to get to the Wen, to cross the chalk-ridge once more, and, at a point where I never crossed it before. Coming through the Weald I found the corn *very good*; and, low as the ground is, wet as it is, cold as it is, there will be very little of the wheat which will not be housed before Saturday night. All the corn is good, and the barley excellent. Not far from BOUGH-BEACH, I saw two oak trees, one of which was, they told me, more than thirty feet round, and the other more than twenty-seven; but they have been hollow for half a century. They are not much bigger than the oak upon Tilford Green, if any. I mean in the trunk; but they are hollow, while that tree is sound in all its parts, and growing still. I have had a most beautiful ride through the Weald. The day is very hot; but I have been in the shade; and my horse's feet very often in the rivulets and wet lanes. In one place I rode above a mile completely arched over by the boughs of the underwood, growing in the banks of the lane. What an odd taste that man must have who prefers a turnpike-road to a lane like this!

Very near to Westerham there are hops; and I have seen now and then a little bit of hop garden, even in the Weald. Hops will grow well where lucerne will grow well; and lucerne will grow well where there is a rich top and a dry bottom. When therefore you see hops in the Weald, it is on the side of some hill, where there is sand or stone at bottom, and not where there is real clay beneath. There appear to be hops, here and there, all along from nearly at Dover to Alton, in Hampshire. You find them all along Kent; you find them at Westerham; across at Worth, in Sussex; at Godstone, in Surrey; over to the north of Merrow Down, near Guildford; at GODALMING; under the Hog's-back, at Farnham; and all along that way to Alton. But there I think, they end. The whole face of the country seems to rise when you get just beyond ALTON, and to keep up. Whether you look to the north, the south, or west, the land seems to rise, and the hops cease, till you come again away to the north-west, in Herefordshire.

Kensington,
Saturday night 6 Sept.

Here I close my day, at the end of forty-four miles. In coming up the chalk hill from Westerham, I prepared myself for the red stiff clay-like loam, the big yellow flints and the meadows; and I found them all. I have now gone over this chalk-ridge in the following places: at COOMBE in the North-West of Hampshire; I mean the North-West corner, the very extremity of the county. I have gone over it at ASHMANSWORTH, or HIGHCLERE, going from Newbury to Andover; at KINGSCLERE, going from NEWBURY to WINCHESTER; at ROPLEY, going from ALRESFORD to Selbourne; at DIPPINGHALL, going from Crondall to Thursly; at MERROW, going from CHERTSEY to CHILWORTH; at REIGATE; at WESTERHAM, and then, between these, at GODSTONE; at SEVENOAKS, going from London to BATTLE; at HOLLINGBOURNE, as mentioned above, and at FOLKESTONE. In all these places I have crossed this chalk-ridge. Every where, upon the top of it, I have found a flat, and the soil of all these flats I have found to be a red stiff loam mingled up with big yellow flints. A soil difficult to work; but by no means bad, whether for wood, hops, grass, orchards or corn. I once before mentioned that I was assured that the pasture upon these bleak hills was as rich as that which is found in the North of Wiltshire, in the neighbourhood of SWINDON, where they make some of the best cheese in the kingdom. Upon these hills I have never found the labouring people poor and miserable, as in the rich vales. All is not appropriated where there are coppices and wood, where the cultivation is not so easy and the produce so very large.

After getting up the hill from Westerham, I had a general descent to perform all the way to the Thames. When you get to Beckenham, which is the last parish in Kent, the country begins to assume a cockney-like appearance; all is artificial, and you no longer feel any interest in it. I was anxious to make this journey into Kent, in the midst of harvest, in order that I might *know* the real state of the crops. The result of my observations and my inquiries, is, that the crop is a *full average* crop of every thing except barley, and that the barley yields a great deal more than an average crop. I thought that the beans were very poor during my ride into Hampshire; but I then saw no real bean countries. I have seen such countries now; and I do not think that the beans present us with a bad crop. As to the quality, it is, in no case (except perhaps the barley), equal to that of last year. We had, last year, an Italian summer. When the wheat, or other grain has to *ripen in wet weather*, it will not be *bright*, as it will when it has to ripen in fair weather. It will have a dingy or clouded appearance; and perhaps the flour may not be quite so good. The wheat, in fact, will not be so heavy. In order to enable others to judge, as well as myself, I took samples from the fields as I went along. I took them very fairly, and as often as I thought that there was any material change in the soil or other circumstances. During the ride I took sixteen samples. These are now at the Office of the Register, in Fleet-street, where they may be seen by any gentleman who thinks the information likely to be useful to him. The samples are numbered, and there is a reference pointing out the place where each sample was taken. The opinions that I gather amount to this; that there is an average crop of every thing, and a little more of barley.

Now then we shall see how all this tallies with the schemes, with the intentions and expectations of our matchless gentlemen at Whitehall. These wise men have put forth their views in the '*Courier*' of the 27th of August, and in words which ought never to be forgotten, and which, at any rate shall be recorded here.

'GRAIN – During the *present unsettled state of the weather*, it is impossible for the best informed persons to anticipate upon good grounds what will be the future price of agricultural produce. Should the season even yet prove favourable, for the operations of the harvest, there is every probability of the average price of grain *continuing at that exact price*, which will prove *most conducive to the interests of the corn growers*, and at the same time *encouraging to the agriculture of our colonial possessions*. We do not *speak lightly* on this subject, for we are aware that His *Majesty's Ministers* have been fully alive to the inquiries from all *qualified quarters* as to the effect likely to be produced on the markets from the addition of the present crops to the stock of wheat already on hand. The result of these inquiries is, that in *the highest quarters* there exists *the full expectation*, that towards the month of November, the price of wheat will *nearly approach to seventy shillings*, a price which, while it affords the *extent of remuneration* to the British farmer, *recognized by the corn laws*, will at the same time admit of the sale of the Canadian bonded wheat; and the introduction of this foreign corn, grown by British colonists, will contribute to keeping down our markets, and *exclude foreign grain from other quarters*.'

There is nice gentlemen of Whitehall! What pretty gentlemen they are! '*Envy of surrounding nations*', indeed, to be under command of pretty gentlemen who can make calculations so nice, and put forth predictions so positive upon such a subject! '*Admiration of the world*' indeed, to live under the command of men who can so controul seasons and markets; or, at least, who can so dive into the secrets of trade, and find out the contents of the fields, barns, and ricks, as to be able to balance things so nicely as to cause the Canadian corn to find a market, without injuring the sale of that of the British farmer, and without admitting that of the French farmer and the other farmers of the continent! Happy, too happy, rogues that we are, to be under the guidance of such pretty gentlemen, and right just is it that we should be banished for life, if we utter a word *tending* to bring such pretty gentlemen into contempt.

Let it be observed, that this paragraph *must* have come from Whitehall. This wretched paper is the demi-official organ of the Government. As to the owners of the paper, DANIEL STEWART, that notorious fellow, STREET, and the rest of them, not excluding the BROTHER OF THE GREAT ORACLE, which brother bought, the other day, a share of this vehicle of baseness and folly; as to these fellows, they have no control other than what relates to the expenditure and the receipts of the vehicle. They get their news from the offices of the Whitehall people, and their paper is the mouth-piece of those same people. Mark this, I pray you, reader; and let the French people mark it, too, and then take their revenge for the Waterloo insolence. This being the case, then; this paragraph proceeding from the pretty gentlemen, what a light it throws on their expectations, their hopes, and their fears. They see that wheat at seventy shillings a quarter is *necessary* to them! Ah! pray mark that! They see that wheat at seventy shillings a quarter is necessary to them; and, therefore, they say that wheat will be at seventy shillings a quarter, the price as they call it necessary to remunerate the British farmer. And how do the conjurors at Whitehall know this? Why, they have made full inquiries 'IN QUALIFIED QUARTERS'. And the qualified quarters have satisfied the 'HIGHEST QUARTERS', that, '*towards the month of November*, the price of wheat will nearly approach to *seventy shillings the quarter!*' I wonder what the words towards the 'end of November' may mean. Devil's in't if middle of September is not '*towards* November'; and the wheat, instead of going on towards seventy shillings, is very fast coming down to forty. The beast who wrote this paragraph; the pretty beast; this 'envy of surrounding nations' wrote it on the 27th of August a *soaking wet Saturday!* The pretty beast was not aware, that the next day was going to be fine, and that we were to have only the succeeding Tuesday and half the following Saturday of wet weather until the whole of the harvest should be in. The pretty beast wrote while the rain was spattering against the window; and he did '*not speak lightly*', but was fully aware that the highest quarters, having made inquiries of the qualified quarters, were sure that wheat would be at seventy shillings during the ensuing year. What will be the price of wheat it is impossible for any one to say. I know a gentleman, who is a very good judge of such matters, who is of opinion that the average price of wheat will be *thirty-two shillings* a quarter, or lower, before Christmas; this is not quite half what the *highest quarters* expect, in consequence of the inquiries which they have made of the *qualified quarters*. I do not say, that the average of wheat will come down to thirty-two shillings; but this I know, that at Reading, last Saturday, about *forty-five* shillings was the price; and I hear, that, in Norfolk, the price is *forty-two*. The *highest quarters*, and the infamous London press, will, at any rate, be prettily exposed, before Christmas. Old SIR THOMAS LETHBRIDGE, too, and GAFFER GOOCH, and his base tribe of Pittites at Ipswich; COKE and SUFFIELD, and their crew; all these will be prettily laughed at; nor will that 'tall soul', LORD MILTON, escape being reminded of his profound and patriotic observation relative to '*this self-renovating country*'. No sooner did he see the wheat get up to sixty or seventy shillings than he lost all his alarms; found that all things were right, turned his back on Yorkshire Reformers, and went and toiled for SCARLETT at Peterborough; and discovered, that there was nothing wrong, at last, and that the 'self-renovating country' would triumph over all its difficulties! – So it will, 'tall soul'; it will triumph over all its difficulties: it will renovate itself: it will purge itself of rotten boroughs, of vile borough-mongers, their tools and their stopgaps; it will purge itself of all the villanies which now corrode its heart; it will, in short, free itself from those curses, which the expenditure of eight or nine hundred millions of English money took place in order to make perpetual: it will, in short, become as free from oppression, as easy and as happy as the gallant and sensible nation on the other side of the Channel. This is the sort of renovation, but not renovation by the means of wheat at seventy shillings a quarter. Renovation it will have: it will rouse and will shake from itself curses like the pension which is paid to BURKE's executors. This is the sort of renovation, 'tall soul'; and not wheat at 70*s.* a quarter while it is at twenty-five shillings a quarter in France. Pray observe, reader, how the 'tall soul' *catched* at the rise in the price of wheat: how he *snapped* at it: how quickly he ceased his attacks upon the Whitehall people and upon the System. He thought he had been deceived: he thought that things were coming about again; and so he drew in his horns, and began to talk about the self-renovating country. This was the tone of them *all*. This was the tone of all the borough-mongers; all the friends of the System; all those, who, like LETH-BRIDGE, had begun to be staggered. They had deviated, for a moment, into our path; but they popped back again the moment they saw the price of wheat rise! All the enemies of Reform, all the calumniators of Reformers, all the friends of the System, most anxiously desired a rise in the price of wheat. Mark the curious fact, that all the vile press of London; the whole of that infamous press; that newspapers, magazines, reviews; the whole of the base thing, and a baser surely this world never saw; that the whole of this base thing rejoiced, exulted, crowed over me, and told an impudent lie, in order to have the crowing; crowed, for what? *because wheat and bread were become dear!* A newspaper hatched under a corrupt Priest, a profligate Priest, and recently espoused to the hell of Pall Mall, even this vile thing crowed because wheat and bread had become dear! Now, it is notorious, that, heretofore, every periodical publication in this kingdom was in the constant habit of lamenting, when bread became dear, and of rejoicing, when it became cheap. This is notorious. Nay, it is equally notorious, that this infamous press was everlastingly assailing bakers, and millers, and butchers, for not selling bread, flour, and meat cheaper than they were selling them. In how many hundreds of instances has this infamous press caused attacks to be made by the mob upon tradesmen of this description! All these things are notorious. More-over, notorious it is that, long previous to every harvest, this infamous, this execrable, this beastly press, was engaged in stunning the public with accounts of the *great crop* which was just coming forward! There was always, with this press, a prodigiously large crop. This was invariably the case. It was never known to be the contrary.

Now these things are perfectly well known to every man in England. How comes it, then, reader, that the profligate, the trading, the lying, the infamous press of London, has now totally changed its tone and bias. The base thing never now tells us that there is a great crop or even a good crop. It never now wants cheap bread and cheap wheat and cheap meat. It never now finds fault of bakers and butchers. It now always endeavours to make it appear that corn is dearer than it is. The base '*Morning Herald*', about three weeks ago, not only suppressed the fact of the fall of wheat, but asserted that there had been a rise in the price. Now *why is all this?* That is a great question, reader. That is a very interesting question. Why has this infamous press, which always pursues that which it thinks its own interest; why has it taken this strange turn? This is the reason: stupid as the base thing is, it has arrived at a conviction, that if the price of the produce of the land cannot be kept up to something approaching ten shillings a bushel for good wheat, *the hellish system of funding must be blown up*. The infamous press has arrived at a conviction, that that cheating, that fraudulent system by which this press lives, *must be destroyed* unless the price of corn can be kept up. The infamous traders of the press are perfectly well satisfied, that the *interest of the Debt* must be reduced, unless wheat can be kept up to nearly ten shillings a bushel. Stupid as they are, and stupid as the fellows down at Westminster are, they know very well, that the whole system, stock-jobbers, Jews, cant and all, go to the devil at once, as soon as a deduction is made from the interest of the Debt. Knowing this, they want wheat to sell high; because it has, at last, been hammered into their skulls, that the interest cannot be paid in full, if wheat sells low. Delightful is the dilemma in which they are. Dear bread does not suit their manufactories, and cheap bread does not suit their debt. '*Envy of surrounding nations*', how hard it is that Providence will not enable your farmers to sell dear and the consumers to buy cheap! These are the things that you want. Admiration of the world you are; but have these things you will not. There may be those, indeed, who question whether you yourself know what you want; but, at any rate, if you want these things, you will not have them.

Before I conclude, let me ask the reader to take a look at the *singularity* of the tone and tricks of this Six-Acts Government. Is it not a novelty in the world to see a Government, and in ordinary seasons, too, having its whole soul absorbed in considerations relating to the price of corn. There are our neighbours, the French, who have got a Government engaged in taking military possession of a great neighbouring kingdom to free which from these very French we have recently ex-pended a *hundred and fifty millions of money*. Our neigh-bours have got a Government that is thus engaged, and we have got a Government that employs itself in making incessant '*inquiries in all the qualified quarters*' relative to the price of wheat! Curious employment for a Government! Singular occupation for the Ministers of the GREAT GEORGE! They seem to think nothing of Spain, with its eleven millions of people, being in fact added to France. Wholly insensible do they appear to concerns of this sort, while they sit thinking, day and night, upon the price of the bushel of wheat!

However, they are not, after all, such fools as they appear to be. Despicable, indeed, must be that nation, whose safety or whose happiness does, in any degree, depend on so fluctuating a thing as the price of corn. This is a matter that we must take as it comes. The seasons will be what they will be; and all the calculations of statesmen must be made wholly independent of the changes and chances of seasons. This has always been the case, to be sure. What nation could ever carry on its affairs, if it had to take into consideration the price of corn? Nevertheless, such is the situation of *our Government*, that its very existence, in its present way, depends upon the price of corn. The pretty fellows at Whitehall, if you may say to them: Well, but look at Spain; look at the enormous strides of the French; think of the consequences in case of another war; look, too, at the growing marine of America. See, Mr JENKINSON, see, Mr CANNING, see, Mr HUSKISSON, see, Mr PEEL, and all ye tribe of GRENVILLES, see, what tremendous dangers are gathering together about us! '*Us!* Aye, about *you*; but pray think what tremendous dangers wheat at four shillings a bushel will bring about *us!*' This is the jut. Here lies the whole of it. We laugh at a Government employing itself in making calculations about the price of corn, and in employing its press to put forth market puffs. We laugh at these things; but we should not laugh, if we considered, that it is on the price of wheat that the duration of the power and the profits of these men depends. They know what they want; and they wish to believe themselves, and to make others believe, that they shall have it. I have observed before, but it is necessary to observe again that all those who are for the System, let them be Opposition or Opposition not, feel as Whitehall feels about the price of corn. I have given an instance, in the 'tall soul'; but it is the same with the whole of them, with the whole of those who do not wish to see this infernal System changed. I was informed, and I believe it to be true, that the MARQUIS OF LANSDOWNE said, last April, when the great rise took place in the price of corn, that he had always thought that the cash-measures had but *little effect on prices*; but that he was now satisfied that those measures had *no effect at all on prices!* Now, what is our situation; what is the situation of this country, if we must have the present Ministry, or a Ministry of which the MARQUIS OF LANSDOWNE is to be a Member, if the MARQUIS OF LANSDOWNE did utter these words? And again, I say, that I verily believe he did utter them.

Ours is a Government that now seems to depend very much upon the *weather*. The old type of a ship at sea will not do now, ours is a weather Government; and to know the state of it, we must have recourse to those glasses that the Jews carry about. Weather depends upon the winds, in a great measure; and I have no scruple to say, that the situation of those two RIGHT HONOURABLE youths, that are now gone to the Lakes in the North;

that their situation, next winter, will be rendered very irksome, not to say perilous, by the present *easterly wind*, if it should continue about fifteen days longer. PITT, when he had just made a monstrous issue of paper, and had, thereby, actually put the match which blowed up the old She Devil in 1797 – PITT, at that time, congratulated the nation, that the *wisdom of Parliament had established a solid system of finance*. Any thing but solid it assuredly was; but his system of finance was as worthy of being called solid, as that System of Government which now manifestly depends upon the weather and the winds.

Since my return home (it is now Thursday, 11th September), I have received letters from the EAST, from the NORTH and from the WEST. All tell me that the harvest is very far advanced, and that the crops are free from blight. These letters are not particular, as to the weight of the crop; except that they all say that the barley is excellent. The wind is now coming from the EAST. There is every appearance of the fine weather continuing. Before Christmas, we shall have the wheat down to what will be a *fair average price in future*. I always said that the late rise was a mere puff. It was, in part, a *scarcity* rise. The wheat of 1821 was grown and bad. That of 1822 had to be begun upon in July. The crop has had to last thirteen months and a half. The present crop will have to last only eleven months, or less. The crop of barley, last year, was so very bad; so very small; and the crop of the year before so very bad in quality, that wheat was malted, last year, in great quantities, instead of barley. This year, the crop of barley is prodigious. All these things considered, wheat, if the cash-measures had had no effect, must have been a hundred and forty shillings a quarter, and barley eighty. Yet the first never got to seventy, and the latter never got to forty! And yet there was a man who calls himself a statesman to say that that mere puff of a rise satisfied him, that the cash-measures had never had any effect! Ah! they are all *afraid* to believe in the effect of those cash-measures: they tremble like children at the sight of the rod, when you hold up before them the effect of those cash-measures. Their only hope, is, that I am wrong in my opinions upon that subject; because, if I am right, their System is condemned to speedy destruction!

I thus conclude, for the present, my remarks relative to the harvest and the price of corn. It is the great subject of the day; and the comfort is, that we are now speedily to see whether I be right or whether the MARQUIS of LANSDOWNE be right. As to the infamous London press, the moment the wheat comes down to forty shillings; that is to say, an average Government Return of forty shillings; I will spend *ten pounds* in PLACARDING this infamous press, after the manner in which we used to placard the base and detestable enemies of the QUEEN. This infamous press has been what is vulgarly called '*running its rigs*', for several months past. The *Quakers* have been urging it on, underhanded. They have, I understand, been bribing it pretty deeply, in order to calumniate me, and to favour their own monopoly; but, thank GOD, the cunning knaves have outwitted themselves. They won't play at cards; but they will play at *Stocks*; they will play at Lottery Tickets, and they will play at Mark-lane. They have played a silly game, this time. SAINT SWITHIN, that good old Roman Catholic Saint, seemed to have set a trap for them; he went on, wet, wet, wet, even until the harvest began. Then, after two or three days' sunshine, shocking wet again. the ground soaking, the wheat growing, and the '*Friends*'; the gentle Friends, seeking the Spirit, were as busy amongst the sacks at Mark-lane as the devil in a high wind. In short they bought away, with all the gain of Godliness, *and a little more*, before their eyes. All of a sudden, Saint Swithin took away his clouds; out came the sun; the wind got round to the East; just sun enough and just wind enough; and as the wheat ricks every where rose up, the long jaws of the Quakers dropped down; and their faces of slate became of a darker hue. That sect will certainly be punished, this year; and, let us hope, that such a change will take place in their concerns as will compel a part of them to labour, at any rate; for, at present, their sect is a perfect monster in society; a whole sect, *not one man of whom earns his living by the sweat of his brow*. A sect a great deal worse than the Jews; for some of them *do work*. However, GOD send us the easterly wind, for another fortnight, and we shall certainly see some of this sect at work.

From Kensington, Across Surrey, and Along that County

Having some business at Hartswood, near Reigate, I intended to come off this morning on horseback, along with my son Richard, but it rained so furiously the last night, that we gave up the horse project for to-day, being, by appointment, to be at Reigate by ten o'clock to-day: so that we came off this morning at five o'clock, in a post-chaise, intending to return home and take our horses. Finding, however, that we cannot quit this place till Friday, we have now sent for our horses, though the weather is dreadfully wet. But we are under a farm-house roof, and the wind may whistle and the rain fall as much as they like.

Having done my business at Hartswood to-day about eleven o'clock, I went to a *sale* at a farm, which the farmer is quitting. Here I had a view of what has long been going on all over the country. The farm, which belongs to *Christ's Hospital*, has been held by a man of the name of CHARINGTON, in whose family the lease has been, I hear, a great number of years. The house is hidden by trees. It stands in the Weald of Surrey, close by the *River Mole*, which is here a mere rivulet, though just below this house the rivulet supplies the very prettiest flour-mill I ever saw in my life.

Every thing about this farm-house was formerly the scene of *plain manners* and *plentiful living*. Oak clothes-chests, oak bedsteads, oak chest of drawers, and oak tables to eat on, long, strong, and well supplied with joint stools. Some of the things were many hundreds of years old. But all appeared to be in a state of decay and nearly of *disuse*. There appeared to have been hardly any *family* in that house, where formerly there were, in all probability, from ten to fifteen men, boys, and maids: and, which was the worst of all, there was a *parlour!* Aye, and a *carpet* and *bell-pull* too! One end of the front of this once plain and substantial house had been moulded into a '*parlour*'; and there was the mahogany table, and the fine chairs, and the fine glass, and all as bare-faced upstart as any stock-jobber in the kingdom can boast of. And, there were the decanters, the glasses, the 'dinner-set' of crockery ware, and all just in the true stock-jobber style. And I dare say it has been '*Squire* Charington and the *Miss* Charingtons; and not plain Master Charington, and his son Hodge, and his daughter Betty Charington, all of whom this accursed system has, in all likelihood, transmuted into a species of mock gentle-folks, while it has ground the labourers down into real slaves. Why do not farmers now *feed* and *lodge* their work-people, as they did formerly? Because they cannot keep them *upon so little* as they give them in wages. This is the real cause of the change. There needs no more to prove that the lot of the working classes has become worse than it formerly was. This fact alone is quite sufficient to settle this point. All the world knows, that a number of people, boarded in the same house, and at the same table, can, with as good food, be boarded much cheaper than those persons divided into twos, threes, or fours, can be boarded. This is a well-known truth: therefore, if the farmer now shuts his pantry against his labourers, and pays them wholly in money, is it not clear, that he does it because he thereby gives them a living *cheaper* to him; that is to say, a *worse* living than formerly? Mind he has *a house* for them; a kitchen for them to sit in, bed rooms for them to sleep in, tables, and stools, and benches, of everlasting duration. All these he has: all these *cost him nothing*; and yet so much does he gain by pinching them in wages that he lets all these things remain as of no use, rather than feed labourers in the house. Judge, then, of the *change* that has taken place in the condition of these labourers! And, be astonished, if you can, at the *pauperism* and the *crimes* that now disgrace this once happy and moral England.

The land produces, on an average, what it always produced; but, there is a new distribution of the produce. This 'Squire Charington's father used, I dare say, to sit at the head of the oak-table along with his men, say grace to them, and cut up the meat and the pudding. He might take a cup of *strong beer* to himself, when they had none; but, that was pretty nearly all the difference in their manner of living. So that *all* lived well. But, the *'Squire* had many *wine-decanters* and *wine-glasses* and 'a *dinner set'*, and a *'breakfast set'*, and *'desert knives'*; and these evidently imply carryings on and a consumption that must of necessity have greatly robbed the long oak table if it had remained fully tenanted. That long table could not share in the work of the decanters and the dinner set. Therefore, it became almost untenanted; the labourers retreated to hovels, called cottages; and, instead of board and lodging, they got money; so little of it as to enable the employer to drink wine; but, then, that he might not reduce them to *quite starvation*, they were enabled to come to him, in the *king's name*, and demand food as *paupers*. And, now mind, that which a man receives in the *king's name*, he knows well he has *by force*; and it is not in nature that he should *thank* any body for it, and least of all the party *from whom it is forced*. Then, if this sort of force be insufficient to obtain him *enough* to eat and to keep him warm, is it surprising, if he think it *no great offence against God* (who created no man to starve) to use *another sort of force* more within his own controul? Is it, in short, surprising, if he resort to *theft* and *robbery*?

This is not only the *natural* progress, but it *has been* the progress in England. The blame is not justly imputed to 'SQUIRE CHARINGTON and his like: the blame belongs to the infernal stock-jobbing system. There was no reason to expect, that farmers would not endeavour to keep pace, in point of show and luxury, with fund-holders, and with all the tribes that *war* and *taxes* created. Farmers were not the authors of the mischief; and *now* they are compelled to shut the labourers out of their houses, and to pinch them in their wages, in order to be able to pay their own taxes; and, besides this, the manners and the principles of the working class are so changed, that a sort of self-preservation bids the farmer (especially in some counties) to keep them from beneath his roof.

I could not quit this farm house without reflecting on the thousands of scores of bacon and thousands of bushels of bread that had been eaten from the long oak-table which, I said to myself, is now perhaps, going, at last, to the bottom of a bridge that some stock-jobber will stick up over an artificial river in his cockney-garden. '*By – it shant*,' said I, almost in a real passion: and so I requested a friend to buy it for me; and if he do so, I will take it to Kensington, or to Fleet-street, and keep it for the good it has done in the world.

When the old farm-houses are down (and down they must come in time) what a miserable thing the country will be! Those that are now erected are mere painted shells, with a Mistress within, who is stuck up in a place she calls a *parlour*, with, if she have children, the 'young ladies and gentlemen' about her: some showy chairs and a sofa (a *sofa* by all means): half a dozen prints in gilt frames hanging up: some swinging book-shelves with novels and tracts upon them: a dinner brought in by a girl that is perhaps better 'educated' than she: two or three nick-nacks to eat instead of a piece of bacon and a pudding: the house too neat for a dirty-shoed carter to be allowed to come into; and every thing proclaiming to every sensible beholder, that there is here a constant anxiety to make a *show* not warranted by the reality. The children (which is the worst part of it) are all too clever to *work*: they are all to be *gentlefolks*. Go to plough! Good God! What, 'young gentlemen' go to plough! They become *clerks*, or some skimmy-dish thing or other. They flee from the dirty *work* as cunning horses do from the bridle. What misery is all this! What a mass of materials for producing that general and *dreadful convulsion* that must, first or last, come and blow this funding and jobbing and enslaving and starving system to atoms!

I was going, to-day, by the side of a plat of ground, where there was a very fine flock of *turkeys*. I stopped to admire them, and observed to the owner how fine they were, when he answered, 'We owe them entirely *to you*, Sir; for, we never raised one till we read your COTTAGE ECONOMY.' I then told him, that we had, this year, raised two broods at Kensington, one black and one white, one of *nine* and one of *eight*; but, that, about three weeks back, they appeared to become dull and pale about the head; and, that, therefore, I sent them to a farm house, where they recovered instantly, and the broods being such a contrast to each other in point of colour, they were now, when prowling over a grass field amongst the most agreeable sights that I had ever seen. I intended of course, to let them get their full growth at Kensington, where they were in a grass plat about fifteen yards square, and where I thought that the feeding of them, in great abundance, with lettuces and other greens from the garden, together with grain, would carry them on to perfection. But, I found that I was wrong; and that, though you may raise them to a certain size, in a small place and with such management, they then, if so much confined, begin to be sickly. Several of mine began actually *to droop:* and, the very day they were sent into the country, they became as gay as ever, and, in three days, all the colour about their heads came back to them.

This town of Reigate had, in former times, a PRIORY, which had considerable estates in the neighbourhood; and this is brought to my recollection by a circumstance which has recently taken place in this very town. We all know how long it has been the fashion for us to take it for *granted*, that the monasteries were *bad things*; but, of late, I have made some hundreds of thousands of very good Protestants *begin to suspect*, that monasteries were better than *poor-rates*, and that monks and nuns, who *fed the poor*, were better than sinecure and pension men and women, who *feed upon the poor*. But, how came the monasteries? How came this that was at Reigate, for instance? Why, it was, if I recollect correctly, *founded by a Surrey gentleman*, who gave this spot and other estates to it, and who, as was usual, provided that masses were to be said in it for his soul and those of others, and that it should, as usual, give aid to the poor and needy.

Now, upon the face of the transaction, what *harm* could this do the community? On the contrary, it must, one would think, do it *good*; for here was this estate given to a set of landlords who *never could quit the spot*; who could *have no families*; who could *save no money*; who could *hold no private property*; who could *make no will*; who must *spend all their income at Reigate and near it*; who, as was the custom, fed the poor, administered to the sick, and taught some, at least, of the people, *gratis*. This, upon the face of the thing, seems to be a very good way of disposing of a rich man's estate.

'Aye, but,' it is said, '*he left his estate away from his relations.*' That is not *sure*, by any means. The *contrary is*

fairly to be presumed. Doubtless, it was the custom for
Catholic Priests, before they took their leave of a dying
rich man, to advise him to think of the *Church and the
Poor*; that is to say to exhort him to *bequeath something to
them*; and this has been made a monstrous charge against
that Church. It is surprising how blind men are, when
they have *a mind to be blind*; what despicable dolts they
are, when they desire to be cheated. We, of the Church
of England, must have a special deal of good sense and
of modesty, to be sure, to rail against the Catholic Church
on this account, when our own Common Prayer Book,
copied from an act of Parliament, *commands our Parsons
to do just the same thing!*

Ah! say the Dissenters, and particularly the Unitarians;
that queer sect, who will have all the wisdom in the
world to themselves; who will believe and won't believe; who will be Christians and who won't have *a
Christ*; who will laugh at you, if you believe in the
Trinity, and who would (if they could) boil you in oil if
you do not believe in the Resurrection: 'Oh!' say the
Dissenters, 'we know very well, that your *Church Parsons*
are commanded to get, if they can, dying people to give
their money and estates to the Church and *the poor*, as they
call the concern, though the *poor*, we believe, come in
for very little which is got in this way. But, what is *your
Church*? We are the real Christians; and we, upon our
souls, never play such tricks; never, no never, terrify old
women out of their stockings full of guineas.' 'And, as
to us,' say the Unitarians, 'we, the most *liberal* creatures upon earth; we, whose virtue is indignant at the
tricks by which the Monks and Nuns got legacies from

dying people to the injury of heirs and other relations; we, who are the really enlightened, the truly consistent, the benevolent, the disinterested, the exclusive patentees of the SALT OF THE EARTH, which is sold only at, or by express permission from our old and original warehouse and manufactory, Essex-street, in the Strand, first street on the left, going from Temple Bar towards Charing Cross; we defy you to show that Unitarian Parsons . . .'

Stop your protestations and hear my Reigate anecdote, which, as I said above, brought the recollection of the OLD PRIORY into my head. The readers of the Register heard me, several times, some years ago, mention Mr BARON MASERES, who was, for a great many years, what they call *Cursitor Baron of the Exchequer*. He lived partly in London and partly at Reigate, for more, I believe, than half a century; and he died, about two years ago, or less, leaving, I am told, *more than a quarter of a million of money*. The Baron came to see me, in Pall Mall, in 1800. He always came frequently to see me, wherever I was in London; not by any means omitting to *come to see me in Newgate*, where I was imprisoned for two years, with a thousand pounds fine and seven years heavy bail, for having expressed my indignation at the flogging of Englishmen, in the heart of England, under a guard of German bayonets; and, to Newgate he always came in *his wig and gown*, in order, as he said, to show his abhorrence of the sentence. I several times passed a week, or more, with the Baron at his house, at Reigate, and might have passed many more, if my time and taste would have permitted me to accept of his invitations. Therefore, I knew the Baron well. He was a most conscientious man; he was when I first knew him, still a very clever man; he retained all his faculties to a very great age; in 1815, I think it was, I got a letter from him, written in a firm hand, correctly as to grammar, and ably as to matter, and he must then have been *little short of ninety*. He never was a bright man; but had always been a very sensible, just and humane man, and a man too who always cared a great deal for the public good; and he was the only man that I ever heard of, who *refused to have his salary augmented*, when an augmentation was offered, and when all other such *salaries were augmented*. I had heard of this: I asked him about it when I saw him again; and he said: 'There was no *work* to be added, and I saw no justice in adding to the salary. It must,' added he, 'be *paid by somebody*, and the more I take, the less that somebody must have.'

He did not save money for money's sake. He saved it because his habits would not let him spend it. He kept a house in Rathbone Place, chambers in the Temple, and his very pretty place at Reigate. He was by no means stingy, but his *scale* and *habits* were cheap. Then, consider, too, *a bachelor of nearly a hundred years old*. His father left him a fortune, his brother (who also died a *very old* bachelor), left him another; and the money lay in the funds, and it went on doubling itself over and over again, till it became that immense mass which we have seen above, and which, when the Baron was making his will, he had neither Catholic priest nor Protestant parson to exhort him to leave to the church and the poor, instead of his relations; though, as we shall presently see, he had somebody else to whom to leave his great heap of money.

The Baron was a most implacable enemy of the Catholics, as Catholics. There was rather a peculiar reason for this, his grandfather having been a *French Hugonot* and having fled with his children to England, at the time of the revocation of the Edict of Nantz. The Baron was a very humane man; his humanity made him assist to support the French emigrant priests; but, at the same time, he caused *Sir Richard Musgrave's book against the Irish Catholics to be published at his own expense*. He and I never agreed upon this subject; and this subject was, with him, a *vital* one. He had no asperity in his nature; he was naturally all gentleness and benevolence; and, therefore, he never *resented* what I said to him on this subject (and which nobody else ever, I believe, ventured to say to him): but, he did not like it; and he liked it the less because I certainly beat him in the argument. However this was long before he visited me in Newgate: and it never produced (though the dispute was frequently revived) any difference in his conduct towards me, which was uniformly friendly to the last time I saw him before his memory was gone.

There was great excuse for the Baron. From his very birth he had been taught to hate and abhor the Catholic religion. He had been told, that his father and mother had been driven out of France by the Catholics: and there was *that mother* dinning this in his ears, and all manner of horrible stories along with it, during all the tender years of his life. In short, the prejudice made part of his very frame. In the year 1803, in August, I think it was, I had gone down to his house on a Friday, and was there on a Sunday. After dinner he and I and his brother walked to the PRIORY, as is still called the mansion house, in the dell at Reigate, which is now occupied by LORD EASTNOR, and in which a Mr BIRKET, I think, then lived. After coming away from the PRIORY, the Baron (whose native place was Betchworth, about two or three miles from Reigate) who knew the history of every house and every thing else in this part of the country, began to tell me why the place was called *the Priory*. From this he came to the *superstition* and *dark ignorance* that induced people to found monasteries; and he dwelt particularly on the *injustice to heirs and relations*; and he went on, in the usual Protestant strain, and with all the bitterness of which he was capable, against those *crafty priests*, who thus *plundered families* by means of the influence which they had over people in their dotage, or who were naturally weak-minded.

Alas! poor Baron! he does not seem to have at all foreseen what was to become of his own money! What would he have said to me, if I had answered his observations by predicting, that HE would give his great mass of money to a *little parson* for that *parson's own private use*; leave only a mere pittance to *his own relations*; leave the little parson his house in which we were *then sitting* (along with all his other real property); that the little parson would come into the house and *take possession*; and that his own relations (two nieces) would *walk out!* Yet, all this has actually taken place, and that, too, after the poor old Baron's four score years of jokes about the tricks of *Popish* priests, practised, in the *dark ages*, upon the *ignorant* and *superstitious* people of Reigate.

When I first knew the Baron he was a staunch *Church*

of England man. He went to church every Sunday once, at least. He used to take me to Reigate church; and I observed, that he was very well versed in his prayer book. But, a decisive proof of his zeal as a Church of England man is, that he settled an annual sum on the incumbent of Reigate, in order to induce him to preach, or pray (I forget which), in the church, twice on a Sunday, instead of once; and, in case this additional preaching, or praying, were not performed in Reigate church, the annuity was to go (and sometimes it does now go) to the poor of an *adjoining* parish, and *not to those of Reigate*, lest I suppose, the parson, the overseers, and other rate-payers, might happen to think that the Baron's annuity would be better laid out in food for the bodies than for the souls of the poor; or, in other words, lest the money should be taken annually and added to the poor-rates to ease the purses of the farmers.

It did not, I dare say, occur to the poor Baron (when he was making this settlement), that he was now *giving money to make a church parson put up additional prayers*, though he had, all his lifetime, been laughing at those, who, in the *dark* ages, gave money, for this purpose, to Catholic priests. Nor did it, I dare say, occur, to the Baron, that, in his contingent settlement of the annuity on the poor of an *adjoining parish*, he as good as declared his opinion, that he *distrusted the piety* of the parson, the overseers, the churchwardens, and, indeed, of all the people of Reigate: yes, at the very moment that he was providing additional prayers for them, he in the very same parchment, put a provision, which clearly showed that he was thoroughly convinced that they, overseers, church-wardens, people, parson and all, *loved money better than prayers*.

What was this, then? Was it hypocrisy; was it ostentation? No: mistake. The Baron thought that those who could not go to church in the morning ought to have an opportunity of going in the afternoon. He was aware of the power of money; but, when he came to make his obligatory clause, he was compelled to do that which reflected great discredit on the very church and religion, which it was his object to honour and uphold.

However, the Baron *was* a staunch churchman as this fact clearly proves: several years he had become what they call an *Unitarian*. The first time (I think) that I perceived this, was in 1812. He came to see me in Newgate, and he soon began to talk *about religion*, which had not been much his habit. He went on at a great rate, laughing about the Trinity, and I remember that he repeated the Unitarian distich, which makes *a joke* of the idea of there being a devil, and which they all repeat to you, and at the same time laugh and look as cunning and as priggish as jack-daws; just as if they were wiser than all the rest in the world! I hate to hear the conceited and disgusting prigs, seeming to take it for granted, that they only are wise, because others *believe* in the incarnation, without being able to reconcile it to *reason*. The prigs don't consider, that there is no more *reason* for the *resurrection* than for the *incarnation*; and yet having taken it into their heads to *come up again*, they would murder you, if they dared, if you were to deny the *resurrection*. I do most heartily despise this priggish set for their conceit and impudence; but, seeing that they want *reason* for the incarnation; seeing that they will have *effects*, here, ascribed to none but *usual causes*, let me put a question or two to them.

1. *Whence* comes the *white clover*, that comes up and covers all the ground, in America, where hard-wood trees, after standing for thousands of years, have been burnt down?
2. *Whence* come (in similar cases as to self-woods) the hurtle-berries in some places, and the raspberries in others?
3. *Whence* come fish in new made places where no fish have ever been put?
4. *What causes* horse-hair to become living things?
5. *What causes* frogs to come in drops of rain, or those drops of rain to turn to frogs, the moment they are on the earth?
6. *What causes* musquitoes to come in rain water caught in a glass, covered over immediately with oil paper, tied down and so kept till full of these winged torments?
7. *What causes* flounders, real little *flat fish*, brown on one side, white on the other, mouth side-ways, with tail, fins, and all, *leaping alive*, in the INSIDE of a rotten sheep's and of every rotten sheep's, LIVER?

There, prigs; answer these questions. Fifty might be given you; but these are enough. Answer these. I suppose you will not deny the facts? They are all notoriously true. The *last*, which of itself would be quite enough for you, will be attested on oath, if you like it, by any farmer, ploughman, and shepherd, in England. Answer this question 7, or hold your conceited gabble about the '*impossibility*' of that which I need not here name.

Men of sense do not attempt to discover that which it is *impossible* to discover. They leave things pretty much as they find them; and take care, at least, not to make changes of any sort, without very evident necessity. The poor Baron, however, appeared to be quite eaten up with his '*rational* Christianity'. He talked like a man who has made a *discovery* of his *own*. He seemed as pleased as I, when I was a boy, used to be, when I had just found a rabbit's stop, or a black-bird's nest full of young ones. I do not recollect what I said upon this occasion. It is most likely that I said nothing in contradiction to him. I saw the Baron many times after this, but I never talked with him about religion.

Before the summer of 1822, I had not seen him for a year or two, perhaps. But, in July of that year, on a very hot day, I was going down *Rathbone Place*, and, happening to cast my eye on the Baron's house, I knocked at the door to ask how he was. His man servant came to the door, and told me that his master was at dinner. 'Well,' said I, 'never mind; give my best respects to him.' But, the servant (who had always been with him since I knew him) begged me to come in, for that he was sure his master would be glad to see me. I thought, as it was likely that I might never see him again, I would go in. The servant announced me, and the Baron said, 'Beg him to walk in.' In I went, and there I found the Baron *at dinner*; but *not quite alone*; nor without *spiritual* as well as carnal and vegetable nourishment before him: for, there, on the opposite side of his *vis-a-vis* dining table, sat that nice, neat, straight, prim piece of mortality, commonly called the REVEREND ROBERT FELLOWES, who was the *Chaplain to the unfortunate Queen* until *Mr Alderman Wood's son* came to supply his place, and who was now, I could clearly see, *in a fair way enough*. I had dined, and so I let them dine on. The Baron was become quite a child, or worse, as to *mind*, though he ate as heartily as I ever saw him, and he was always a great eater. When his servant said, 'Here is Mr Cobbett, Sir;' he said, 'How do you do, Sir? I have read much of your writings, Sir; but *never had the pleasure to see your person before.*' After a time I made him recollect me; but, he, directly after, being about to relate something about America, turned towards me, and said, '*Were you ever in America,* Sir?' But, I must mention one proof of the state of his mind. Mr FELLOWES asked me about the news from Ireland, where the people were then in a *state of starvation* (1822), and I answering that, *it was likely that many of them would actually be starved to death*, the Baron, quitting his green goose and green pease, turned to me and said, '*Starved*, Sir! Why don't they go to *the parish?*' 'Why,' said I, 'you know, Sir, that there are no poor-rates in Ireland.' Upon this he exclaimed, 'What! no poor-rates in Ireland? Why not? I did not know that; I can't think how that can be.' And then he rambled on in a childish sort of way.

At the end of about half an hour, or, it might be more, I shook hands with the poor old Baron for the last time, well convinced that I should never see him again, and not less convinced, that I had seen his *heir*. He died in about a year or so afterwards, left to his own family about 20,000*l.*, and to his *ghostly guide*, the HOLY ROBERT FELLOWES, all the rest of his immense fortune, which, as I have been told, amounts to more than a quarter of a million of money.

Now, the public will recollect that, while Mr FEL-LOWES was at the Queen's, he was, in the public papers, charged with being an *Unitarian*, at the same time that he officiated *as her chaplain*. It is also well known, that he never publicly contradicted this. It is, besides, the general belief at Reigate. However, this we know well, that he is a *parson*, of one sort or the other, and that he is not *a Catholic priest*. That is enough for me. I see this poor, foolish old man leaving a monstrous mass of money to this little Protestant *parson*, whom he had *not even known* more, I believe, than about three or four years. When the will was made I cannot say. I know nothing at all about that. I am supposing that all was perfectly fair; that the Baron had his senses when he made his will; that he clearly meant to do that which he did. But, then, I must insist, that, if he had left the money to a *Catholic priest*, to be by him expended on the endowment of a convent, wherein to say masses and to feed and teach the poor, it would have been a more sensible and public-spirited part in the Baron, much more beneficial to the town and environs of Reigate, and beyond all measure more honourable to his own memory.

Chilworth, Friday Evening,
21st Oct. 1825

It has been very fine to-day. Yesterday morning there was *snow* on Reigate Hill, enough to look white from where we were in the valley. We set off about half past one o'clock, and came all down the valley, through Buckland, Betchworth, Dorking, Sheer and Aldbury, to this place. Very few prettier rides in England, and the weather beautifully fine. There are more meeting-houses than churches in the vale, and I have heard of no less than five people, in this vale, who have gone crazy on account of religion.

To-morrow we intend to move on towards the West; to take a look, just a look, at the *Hampshire parsons* again. The turnips *seem* fine; but they cannot be large. All other things are very fine indeed. Every thing seems to prognosticate a hard winter. All the country people say that it will be so.

From Chilworth, in Surrey, to Winchester

Thursley, four miles from Godalming, Surrey,
Sunday Evening, 23d October, 1825

We set out from Chilworth to-day about noon. This is a little hamlet, lying under the South side of St Martha's Hill; and, on the other side of that hill, a little to the North West, is the town of GUILDFORD, which (taken with its environs) I, who have seen so many, many towns, think the prettiest, and, taken all together, the most agreeable and most happy-looking, that I ever saw in my life. Here are hill and dell in endless variety. Here are the chalk and the sand, vieing with each other in making beautiful scenes. Here is a navigable river and fine meadows. Here are woods and downs. Here is something of every thing but *fat marshes* and their skeleton making *agues*. The vale, all the way down to Chilworth from Reigate, is very delightful. – We did not go to Guildford, nor did we cross the *River Wey*, to come through GODALMING; but bore away to our left, and came through the village of Hambleton, going first to HASCOMB, to show Richard the South Downs from that high land, which looks Southward over the *Wealds* of Surrey and Sussex, with all their fine and innumerable oak trees. Those that travel on turnpike roads know nothing of England. – From Hascomb to Thursley almost the whole way is across fields, or commons, or along narrow lands. Here we see the people without any disguise or affectation. Against a *great road* things are made for *show*. Here we see them *without any show*. And here we gain real knowledge as to their situation. – We crossed to-day, three turnpike roads, that from Guildford to Horsham, that from Godalming to Worthing, I believe, and that from Godalming to Chichester.

Thursley,
Wednesday, 26th Oct.

The weather has been beautiful ever since last Thursday morning; but, there has been a white frost every morning, and the days have been coldish. *Here*, however, I am quite at home in a room, where there is one of my *American Fire-Places*, bought, by my host, of MR JUDSON OF KENSINGTON, who has made many a score of families comfortable, instead of sitting shivering in the cold. At the house of the gentleman, whose house I am now in, there is a good deal of *fuel-wood*; and here I see, in the parlours, those fine and cheerful fires that make a great part of the happiness of the Americans. But, these fires are to be had only in this sort of fire-place. Ten times the fuel; nay, no quantity, would effect the same object, in any other fire-place. It is equally good for *coal* as for wood; but, for *pleasure*, a wood-fire is the thing. There is, round about almost every gentleman's or great farmer's house, more wood suffered to rot every year, in one shape or another, than would make (with this fire-place) a couple of rooms constantly warm, from October to June.

Here, peat, turf, saw-dust, and wood, are burnt in these fire-places. My present host has *three* of the fire-places. – Being out a-coursing to-day, I saw *a queer-looking building* upon one of the thousands of hills that nature has tossed up in endless variety of form round the skirts of the lofty *Hindhead*. This building is, it seems, called a *Semaphore*, or *Semiphare*, or something of that sort. What this word may have been hatched out of I cannot say; but it means *a job*, I am sure. To call it an *alarm-post* would not have been so convenient; for, people not endued with Scotch *intellect*, might have wondered *why* the devil we should have to pay for *alarm-posts*; and might have thought, that, with all our *'glorious victories'*, we had 'brought our hogs to a fine market', if our *dread of the enemy* were such as to induce us to have *alarm posts* all over the country! Such unintellectual people might have thought that we had *'conquered* France by the *immortal* Wellington', to little purpose, if we were still in such fear as to build alarm-posts; and they might, in addition, have observed, that, for many hundred of years, England stood in need of neither signal posts nor standing army of mercenaries; but relied safely on the courage and public spirit of the people themselves. By calling the thing by an outlandish name, these reflections amongst the unintellectual are obviated. *Alarm-post* would be a nasty name; and it would puzzle people exceedingly, when they saw one of these at a place like ASHE, a little village on the north side of the chalk-ridge (called the hog's back) going from Guildford to Farnham! What can this be *for*? Why are these expensive things put up all over the country? Respecting the movements of *whom* is wanted this *alarm-*

system? Will *no member ask this in parliament?* Not one: not a man: and yet it is a thing to ask about. Ah! it is in vain, THING, that you thus are *making your preparations*; in vain that you are setting your trammels. The DEBT, the blessed debt, that best ally of the people, will break them all; will snap them, as the hornet does the cobweb; and, even these very '*Semaphores*', contribute towards the force of that ever-blessed debt. Curious to see how things *work!* The '*glorious* revolution', which was made for the avowed purpose of maintaining the *Protestant ascendancy*, and which was followed by such terrible persecution of the Catholics; that '*glorious*' affair, which set aside a race of kings, *because they were Catholics*, served as the *precedent* for the American revolution, also called '*glorious*', and this second revolution *compelled the successors of the makers of the first, to begin to cease their persecutions of the Catholics!* Then, again, the debt was made to raise and keep armies on foot to prevent *reform of parliament*, because, as it was feared by the Aristocracy, reform would have humbled them; and this debt, created for this purpose, is fast sweeping the Aristocracy out of their estates, as a clown, with his foot, kicks field-mice out of their nests. There was a hope, that the debt could have been *reduced* by *stealth*, as it were; that the Aristocracy could have been *saved in this* way. That hope now *no longer exists*. In all likelihood the funds will keep going down. What is to prevent this, if the *interest of Exchequer Bills be raised*, as the broad sheet tells us it is to be? What! the funds fall in *time of peace*; and *the French funds not fall*, in time of peace! However, it will all happen *just as it ought to happen*. Even the next session of parliament will bring out matters of some interest. The thing is now working in the surest possible way.

The great business of life, in the country, appertains, in some way or other, to the *game*, and especially at this time of the year. If it were not for the game, a country life would be like an *everlasting honey-moon*, which would, in about half a century, put an end to the human race. In *towns*, or large villages, people make a shift to find the means of rubbing the rust off from each other by a vast variety of sources of contest. A couple of wives meeting in the street, and giving each other a wry look, or a look not quite civil enough, will, if the parties be hard pushed for a ground of contention, do pretty well. But in the country, there is, alas! no such resource. Here are no walls for people to take of each other. Here they are so placed as to prevent the possibility of such lucky local contact. Here is more than room of every sort, elbow, leg, horse, or carriage, for them all. Even *at Church* (most of the people being in the meeting-houses) the pews are surprisingly too large. Here, therefore, where all circumstances seem calculated to cause never-ceasing concord with its accompanying dullness, there would be no relief at all, were it not for the *game*. This, happily, supplies the place of all other sources of alternate dispute and reconciliation; it keeps all in life and motion, from the lord down to the hedger. When I see two men, whether in a market-room, by the way-side, in a parlour, in a church yard, or even in the church itself, engaged in manifestly deep and most momentous discourse, I will, if it be any time between September and February, bet *ten to one*, that it is, in some way or other, about *the game*.

The wives and daughters hear so much of it, that they inevitably get engaged in the disputes; and thus are all kept in a state of vivid animation. I should like very much to be able to take a spot, a circle of 12 miles in diameter, and take an exact account of all the *time* spent by each individual, above the age of *ten* (that is the age they begin at), in *talking*, during the game season of one year, about *the game* and about *sporting exploits*. I verily believe that it would amount, upon an average, to *six times* as much as *all the other talk put together*; and, as to the *anger*, the *satisfaction*, the *scolding*, the *commendation*, the *chagrin*, the *exultation*, the *envy*, the *emulation*, where are there any of these in the country, unconnected with *the game?*

There is, however, an important distinction to be made between *hunters* (including coursers) and *shooters*. The latter are, as far as relates to their exploits, a disagreeable class, compared with the former; and the reason of this is, their doings are almost wholly *their own*; while, in the case of the others, the achievements are the property of *the dogs*. Nobody likes to hear another talk *much* in praise of his own acts, unless those acts have a manifest tendency to produce some good to the hearer; and shooters do talk *much* of their own exploits, and those exploits rather tend to *humiliate* the hearer. Then, a *great shooter* will, nine times out of ten, go so far as almost to *lie a little*; and, though people do not tell him of it, they do not like him the better for it; and he but too frequently discovers that they do not believe him: whereas, hunters are mere followers of the dogs, as mere *spectators*; their praises, if any are called for, are bestowed on the greyhounds, the hounds, the fox, the hare, or the horses. There is a little rivalship in the riding, or in the behaviour of the horses; but this has so little to do with the *personal merit* of the sportsmen, that it never produces a want of good fellowship in the evening of the day. A shooter who has been *missing* all day, must have an uncommon share of good sense, not to feel mortified while the slaughterers are relating the adventures of that day; and this is what cannot exist in the case of the hunters. Bring me into a room, with a dozen men in it, who have been sporting all day; or, rather let me be in an adjoining room, where I can hear the sound of their voices, without being able to distinguish the words, and I will bet ten to one that I tell whether they be hunters or shooters.

I was once acquainted with a *famous shooter* whose name was WILLIAM EWING. He was a barrister of Philadelphia, but became far more renowned by his gun than by his law cases. We spent scores of days together a shooting, and were extremely well matched, I having excellent dogs and caring little about my reputation as a shot, his dogs being good for nothing, and he caring more about his reputation as a shot than as a lawyer. The fact which I am going to relate respecting this gentleman, ought to be a warning to young men, how they become enamoured of this species of vanity. We had gone about ten miles from our home, to shoot where partridges were said to be very plentiful. We found them so. In the course of a November day, he had, just before dark, shot, and sent to the farm-house, or kept in his bag, *ninety-nine* partridges. He made some few *double shots*, and he might have a *miss* or two, for he sometimes shot when out of my sight, on account of the woods. However, he said that he killed at every shot; and, as he had counted the birds, when we went to dinner at the farm-house and when he cleaned his gun, he, just before sun-set, knew that he had killed *ninety-nine* partridges, every one upon the wing, and a great part of them in woods very thickly set with largish trees. It was a grand achievement; but, unfortunately, he wanted to make it *a hundred*. The sun *was setting*, and, in that country, darkness comes almost at once; it is more like the going out of a candle than that of a fire; and I wanted to be off, as we had a very bad road to go, and as he, being under strict petticoat government, to which he most loyally and dutifully submitted, was compelled to get home that night, taking me with him, the vehicle (horse and gig) being mine. I, therefore, pressed him to come away, and moved on myself towards the house (that of OLD JOHN BROWN, in Bucks county, grandfather of that GENERAL BROWN, who gave some of our whiskered heroes such a rough handling last war, which was waged for the purpose of 'DEPOSING JAMES MADISON'), at which house I would have stayed all night, but from which I was compelled to go by that watchful government, under which he had the good fortune to live. Therefore I was in haste to be off. No: he would kill the *hundredth* bird! In vain did I talk of the bad road and its many dangers for want of moon. The poor partridges, which we had scattered about, were *calling* all around us; and just at this moment, up got one under his feet, in a field in which the wheat was three or four inches high. He shot and *missed*. 'That's it,' said he, running as if to *pick up* the bird. 'What!' said I, 'you don't think you *killed*, do you? Why there is the bird now, not only alive, but *calling*, in that wood'; which was at about a hundred yards distance. He, in that *form of words* usually employed in such cases, asserted that he shot the bird and saw it fall; and I, in much about the same form of words, asserted, that he had *missed*, and that I, with my own eyes, saw the bird fly into the wood. This was too much! To *miss* once out of a hundred times! To lose such a chance of immortality! He was a good-humoured man; I liked him very much; and I could not help feeling for him, when he said, 'Well, *Sir*, I killed the bird; and if you choose to go away and take your dog away, so as to prevent me from *finding* it, you must do it; the dog is *yours*, to be sure.' 'The *dog*,' said I, in a very mild tone, 'why, EWING, there is the spot; and could we not see it, upon this smooth green surface, if it were there?' However, he began to *look about*; and I called the dog, and affected to *join him in the search*. Pity for his weakness got the better of my dread of the bad road. After walking backward and forward many times upon about twenty yards square with our eyes to the ground, looking for what both of us knew was not there, I had *passed him* (he going one way and I the other), and I happened to be turning round just after I had passed him, when I saw him, putting his hand behind him, *take a partridge out of his bag and let it fall upon the ground!* I felt no temptation to detect him, but turned away my head, and kept looking about. Presently he, having returned to the spot where the bird was, called out to me, in a most triumphant tone: '*Here! here!* Come here!' I went up to him, and he, pointing with his finger down to the bird, and looking hard in my face at the same time, said, 'There, Cobbett; I hope that will be a *warning* to you never to be obstinate again!' 'Well,' said I, 'come along': and away we went as merry as larks. When we got to Brown's, he told them the story, triumphed over me most clamorously; and, though he often repeated the story to my face, I never had the heart to let him know, that I knew of the imposition which puerile vanity had induced so sensible and honourable a man to be mean enough to practise. A *professed shot* is, almost always, a very disagreeable brother sportsman. He must, in the first place, have a head rather of the emptiest to *pride himself* upon so poor a talent. Then he is always out of temper, if the game fail, or if he miss it. He never participates in that great delight which all sensible men enjoy at beholding the beautiful action, the docility, the zeal, the wonderful sagacity, of the pointer and the setter. He is always thinking about *himself*; always anxious to surpass his companions. I remember that, once, Ewing and I had lost our dog. We were in a wood, and the dog had gone out, and found a covey in a wheat stubble joining the wood. We had been whistling and calling him for, perhaps, half an hour, or more. When we came out of the wood we saw him pointing, with one foot up; and, soon after, he, keeping his foot and body unmoved, gently turned round his head towards the spot where he heard us, as if to bid us come on, and, when he saw that we saw him, turned his head back again. I was so delighted, that I stopped to look with admiration. Ewing, astonished at my want of alacrity, pushed on, shot one of the partridges, and thought no more about the conduct of the dog than if the sagacious creature had had nothing at all to do with the matter. When I left America, in 1800, I gave this dog to LORD HENRY STUART, who was, when he came home, a year or two afterwards, about to bring him to astonish the sportsmen even in England; but, those of Pennsylvania were resolved not to part with him, and therefore they *stole* him the night before his Lordship came away. Lord Henry had plenty of pointers after his return, and he *saw* hundreds; but always declared, that he never saw any thing approaching in excellence this American dog. For the information of sportsmen I ought to say, that this was a small-headed and sharp-nosed pointer, hair as fine as that of a grey-hound, little and short ears, very light in the body, very long legged, and swift as a good lurcher. I had him a puppy, and he never had any *breaking*, but he pointed staunchly at once; and I am of opinion, that this sort is, in all respects, better than the heavy breed. Mr THORN-TON, (I beg his pardon, I believe he is now a *Knight* of some sort) who was, and perhaps still is, our *Envoy* in *Portugal*, and who, at the time here referred to, was a sort of *partner* with Lord Henry in this famous dog; and gratitude (to the memory of *the dog* I mean,) will, I am sure, or, at least, I hope so, make him bear witness to the truth of my character of him; and, if one could hear an Ambassador *speak out*, I think that Mr THORNTON would acknowledge, that his calling has brought him in pretty close contact with many a man who was possessed of most tremendous political power without possessing half the sagacity, half the understanding, of this dog, and without being a thousandth part so faithful to his trust. I am quite satisfied, that there are as many *sorts* of men as there are of dogs. SWIFT was a man, and so is WALTER the base. But, is the *sort* the same? It cannot be *education* alone that makes the amazing difference that we see. Besides, we see men of the very same rank and riches and education, differing as widely as the pointer does from the pug. The name, *man*, is common to all the sorts, and hence arises very great mischief. What confusion must there be in rural affairs, if there were no names whereby to distinguish hounds, greyhounds, pointers, spaniels, terriers, and sheep dogs, from each other! And, what pretty work, if, without regard to the *sorts* of dogs, men were to attempt to *employ them!* Yet, this is done in the case of *men!* A man is always *a man*; and, without the least regard as to the *sort*, they are promiscuously placed in all kinds of situations. Now, if Mr Brougham, Doctors Birkbeck, Macculloch and Black, and that profound personage, Lord John Russell, will, in their forth-coming 'London University', teach us how to divide men *into sorts*, instead of teaching us to *augment the* CAPITAL *of the nation by making paper-money*, they will render us a real service. That will be *feelosofy* worth attending to. What would be said of the 'Squire who should take a fox-hound out to find partridges for him to shoot at? Yet, would this be *more* absurd than to set a man to law-making who was manifestly formed for the express purpose of sweeping the streets or digging out sewers?

We came over the heath from *Thursley*, this morning, on our way to Winchester. Mr Wyndham's FOX-HOUNDS are coming to Thursley on Saturday. More than three-fourths of all the interesting talk in that neighbourhood, for some days past, has been about this anxiously looked-for event. I have seen no man, or boy, who did not talk about it. There had been a false report about it; the hounds did *not come*; and the anger of the disappointed people was very great. At last, however, the *authentic* intelligence came, and I left them all as happy as if all were young and all just going to be married. An abatement of my pleasure, however, on this joyous occasion was, that I brought away with me *one*, who was as eager as the best of them. RICHARD, though now only 11 years and 6 months old, had, it seems, one fox-hunt, in Hereford-shire, last winter; and he actually has begun to talk rather *contemptuously* of hare hunting. To show me that he is in no *danger*, he has been leaping his horse over banks and ditches by the road side, all our way across the country from Reigate; and he joined with such glee in talking of the expected arrival of the fox-hounds, that I felt some little pain in bringing him away. My engage-ment at Winchester is for Saturday; but, if it had not been so, the *deep and hidden ruts in the heath*, in a wood in the midst of which the hounds are sure to find, and the immense concourse of horsemen that is sure to be assembled, would have made me bring him away. Upon the high, hard and open countries, I should not be afraid for him; but, here the danger would have been greater than it would have been right for me to suffer him to run.

We came hither by the way of WAVERLEY ABBEY and MOORE PARK. On the commons I showed Richard some of my old hunting-scenes, when I was of his age, or younger, reminding him that I was obliged to hunt on foot. We got leave to go and see the grounds at Waverley, where all the old monks' *garden walls* are totally gone, and where the spot is become a sort of lawn. I showed him the spot where the strawberry garden was, and where I, when sent to gather *hautboys*, used to eat every *remarkably fine one*, instead of letting it go to be eaten by Sir ROBERT RICH. I showed him a tree, close by the ruins of the Abbey, from a limb of which I once fell into the river, in an attempt to take the nest of a *crow*, which had artfully placed it upon a branch so far from the trunk as not to be able to bear the weight of a boy eight years old. I showed him an old elm tree, which was hollow even then, into which I, when a very little boy, once saw *a cat go*, that was *as big as a middle-sized spaniel dog*, for relating which I got a great scolding, for standing to which I, at last, got a beating; but, stand to which I still did; I have since many times repeated it, and I would take my oath of it to this day. When in New Brunswick I saw the great wild grey cat, which is there called a *Lucifee*; and it seemed to me to be just such a cat as I had seen at Waverley. I found the ruins not very greatly diminished; but, it is strange how *small* the *mansion* and *ground*, and every thing but the trees, appeared to me. They were all *great to my mind when I saw them last*; and that early impression had remained, whenever I had talked or thought, of the spot; so that when I came to see them again, after seeing the sea and so many other immense things, it seemed as if they had all been *made small*. This was not the case with regard to the *trees*, which are nearly as big here as they are any where else; and, the old cat-elm, for instance, which Richard measured with his whip, is about 16 or 17 feet round.

From Waverley we went to MOORE PARK, once the seat of SIR WILLIAM TEMPLE, and, when I was a very little boy, the seat of a Lady, or a Mrs Temple. Here I showed Richard MOTHER LUDLUM'S HOLE; but, alas! it is not the enchanting place that I knew it, nor that which GROSE describes in his Antiquities! The semicircular paling is gone; the basins, to catch the never-ceasing little stream, are gone; the iron cups, fastened by chains, for people to drink out of, are gone; the pavement all broken to pieces; the seats, for people to sit on, on both sides of the cave, torn up and gone; the stream that ran down a clean paved channel, now making a dirty gutter; and the ground opposite, which was a grove, chiefly of laurels, intersected by closely mowed grass-walks, now become a poor, ragged-looking Alder-Coppice. Near the mansion, I showed Richard the hill, upon which DEAN SWIFT tells us he used to run for exercise, while he was pursuing his studies here; and I would have showed him the garden-seat, under which *Sir William Temple's heart was buried, agreeably to his will*; but, the seat was gone, also the wall at the back of it; and the exquisitely beautiful little lawn in which the seat stood, was turned into a parcel of divers-shaped cockney-clumps, planted according to the strictest rules of artificial and refined vulgarity.

At Waverley, Mr THOMPSON, a merchant of some sort, has succeeded (after the monks) the ORBY HUNTERS and Sir ROBERT RICH. At MOORE PARK, a Mr LAING, a West India planter or merchant, has succeeded the TEMPLES; and at the castle of Farnham, which you see from MOORE PARK, Bishop PRETTYMAN TOMLINE has, at last, after *perfectly regular and due gradations*, succeeded WILLIAM OF WYKHAM! In coming up from Moore Park to Farnham town, I stopped opposite the door of a little old house, where there appeared to be a great parcel of children. 'There, Dick,' said I, 'when I was just such a little creature as that, whom you see in the door-way, I lived in this very house with my grand-mother Cobbett.' He pulled up his horse, and looked *very hard at it*, but said nothing, and on we came.

Winchester,
Sunday noon, Oct. 30

We came away from Farnham about noon on Friday, promising Bishop Prettyman to notice him and his way of living more fully on our return. At Alton we got some bread and cheese at a friend's, and then came to Alresford by *Medstead*, in order to have fine turf to ride on, and to see, on this lofty land that which is, perhaps, the finest *beech-wood* in all England. These high down-countries are not garden plats, like Kent; but they have, from my first seeing them, when I was about *ten*, always been my delight. Large sweeping downs, and deep dells here and there, with villages amongst lofty trees, are my great delight. When we got to Alresford it was nearly dark, and not being able to find a room to our liking, we resolved to go, though in the dark, to EASTON, a village about six miles from Alresford, down by the side of the Hichen River.

Coming from Easton yesterday, I learned that Sir CHARLES OGLE, the eldest son and successor of Sir CHALONER OGLE, has sold to some *General*, his mansion and estate at MARTYR'S WORTHY, a village of the North side of the Hichen, just opposite EASTON. The Ogles had been here for *a couple of centuries* perhaps. They are *gone off now*, 'for good and all', as the country people call it. Well, what I have to say to Sir Charles Ogle upon this occasion is this: 'It was YOU, who moved at the county meeting, in 1817, that *address to the Regent*, which you brought ready engrossed upon parchment, which FLEM-ING, the Sheriff, declared to have been *carried*, though a word of it never was heard by the meeting; which address *applauded the power of imprisonment bill, just then passed*; and the like of which address, YOU WILL NOT IN ALL HUMAN PROBABILITY, EVER AGAIN MOVE IN HAMPSHIRE, and, I hope, NO WHERE ELSE. So, you see, Sir Charles, there is *one consolation*, at any rate.'

I learned, too, that GREAME, a famously loyal 'squire and justice, whose son was, a few years ago, made a *Distributor of Stamps* in this county, was become so modest as to exchange his big and ancient mansion at CHERRITON, or somewhere there, for a very moderate-sized house in the town of ALRESFORD! I saw his *household goods advertised* in the Hampshire newspaper, a little while ago, to be sold *by public auction*. I rubbed my eyes, or, rather, my spectacles, and looked again and again; for *I remembered* the loyal 'Squire; and I, with singular satisfaction, record this change in his scale of existence, which has, no doubt, proceeded solely from that prevalence of mind over matter, which the Scotch *feelosofers* have taken such pains to inculcate, and which makes him flee from greatness as from that which diminishes the quantity of '*intellectual* enjoyment'; and so now he,

> 'Wondering, man can want the larger pile,
> Exults, and owns his cottage with a smile.'

And they really tell me, that his present house is not much bigger than that of my dear, good old grandmother Cobbett. But (and it may be not wholly useless for the 'Squire to know it) she never burnt *candles*; but *rushes* dipped in grease, as I have described them in my *Cottage Economy*; and this was one of the means that she made use of in order to secure a bit of good bacon and good bread to eat, and that made her never give me *potatoes*, cold or hot. No bad hint for the 'Squire, father of the distributor of Stamps. Good bacon is a very nice thing, I can assure him; and, if the quantity be small, it is all the sweeter; provided, however, it be not *too small*. This 'Squire used to be a great friend of *Old George Rose*. But, his patron's *taste* was different from his. George preferred a big house to a little one; and George *began* with a little one, and *ended* with a big one.

Just by ALRESFORD, there was another old friend and supporter of Old George Rose, 'Squire RAWLINSON, whom I remember a very great 'squire in this county.

He is now a *Police-*'squire in London, and is one of those guardians of the Wen, respecting whose proceedings we read eternal columns in the broad-sheet.

This being *Sunday*, I heard, about 7 o'clock in the morning, a sort of a jangling, made by a bell or two in the *Cathedral*. We were getting ready to be off, to cross the country to BURGHCLERE, which lies under the lofty hills at Highclere about 22 miles from this city; but hearing the bells of the cathedral, I took Richard to show him that ancient and most magnificent pile, and particularly to show him the tomb of that famous bishop of Winchester, WILLIAM of WYKHAM; who was the Chancellor and the Minister of the great and glorious King, EDWARD III; who sprang from poor parents in the little village of WYKHAM, three miles from Botley; and who, amongst other great and most munificent deeds, founded the famous College, or School, of Winchester, and also one of the Colleges at Oxford. I told Richard about this as we went from the inn down to the cathedral; and, when I *showed him the tomb*, where the bishop lies on his back, in his Catholic robes, with his mitre on his head, his shepherd's crook by his side, with little children at his feet, their hands put together in a praying attitude, he looked with a degree of inquisitive earnestness that pleased me very much. I took him as far as I could about the Cathedral. The *'service'* was now begun. There is a *dean*, and God knows how many *prebends* belonging to this *immensely* rich bishopric and chapter: and there were, at this *'service'*, *two or three men* and *five or six boys* in white surplices, with a congregation of *fifteen women* and *four men!* Gracious God! If WILLIAM of WYKHAM could,

at that moment, have raised from his tomb! If Saint
Swithin, whose name the cathedral bears, or Alfred
the Great, to whom St Swithin was tutor: if either of
these could have come, and had been told, that *that* was
now what was carried on by men, who talked of the
'*damnable* errors' of those who founded that very church!
But, it beggars one's *feelings* to attempt to find *words*
whereby to express them upon such a subject and such
an occasion. How, then, am I to describe what I felt,
when I yesterday saw in Hyde Meadow, a county
bridwell, standing on the *very spot, where stood the Abbey*
which was founded and endowed by Alfred, which
contained the bones of that maker of the English name,
and also those of the learned monk, St Grimbald, whom
Alfred brought to England *to begin the teaching at Oxford!*

After we came out of the cathedral, Richard said,
'Why, Papa, nobody can build such places *now*, can
they?' 'No, my dear,' said I. 'That building was made
when there were no poor wretches in England, called
paupers; when there were no *poor-rates*; when every
labouring man was clothed in good woollen cloth; and
when all had a plenty of meat and bread and beer.' This
talk lasted us to the inn, where, just as we were going to
set off, it most curiously happened, that a parcel, which
had come from Kensington by the *night coach*, was put
into my hands by the landlord, containing, amongst
other things, a pamphlet, sent to me from Rome, being
an Italian translation of No. 1 of the '*Protestant
Reformation*'. I will here insert the title for the satisfaction
of Doctor Black, who, some time ago, expressed
his utter astonishment, that 'such a work should be

published in the *nineteenth* century'. Why, Doctor? Did you want me to stop till the *twentieth* century? That would have been a little too long, Doctor.

Storia
Della
Riforma Protestante
In Inghilterra ed in Irlanda
La quale Dimostra
Come un tal' avvenimento ha impoverito
E degradato il grosso del popolo in que' paesi
in una serie di lettere indirizzate
A tutti i sensati e guisti inglesi
Da
Guglielmo Cobbett
E
Dall' inglese recate in italiano
Da
Dominico Gregorj.
Roma 1825.
Presso Francesco Bourlie
Con Approvazione.

There, Doctor Black. Write *you* a book that shall be translated into *any* foreign language; and when you have done that, you may *again* call mine '*pig's meat*'.

From Winchester to Burghclere

Burghclere, Monday Morning,
31st October, 1825

We had, or I had, resolved not *to breakfast* at Winchester yesterday: and yet we were detained till nearly noon. But, at last off we came, *fasting*. The turnpike road from Winchester to this place comes through a village, called SUTTON SCOTNEY, and then through WHITCHURCH, which lies on the Andover and London road, through Basingstoke. We did not take the cross-turnpike till we came to Whitchurch. We went to King's Worthy; that is, about two miles on the road from Winchester to London; and then, turning short to our left, came up upon the downs to the north of Winchester race-course. Here, looking back at the city and at the fine valley above and below it, and at the many smaller valleys that run down from the high ridges into that great and fertile valley, I could not help admiring the taste of the ancient kings, who made this city (which once covered all the hill round about, and which contained 92 churches and chapels) a chief place of their residence. There are not many finer spots in England; and if I were to take in a circle of eight or ten miles of semi-diameter, I should say that I believe there is not one so fine. Here are hill, dell, water, meadow, woods, corn-fields, downs; and all of them very fine and very beautifully disposed. This country does not present to us that sort of beauties which we see about Guildford and Godalming, and round the skirts of Hindhead and Blackdown, where the ground lies in the form that the surface-water in a boiling copper would be in, if you could, by word of command, *make it be still*, the variously-shaped bubbles all sticking up; and really, to look at the face of the earth, who can help imagining, that some such process has produced its present form? Leaving this matter to be solved by those who laugh at mysteries, I repeat, that the country round Winchester does not present to us beauties of *this sort*; but of a sort which I like a great deal better. Arthur Young calls the vale between Farnham and Alton *the finest ten miles in* England. Here is a river with fine meadows on each side of it, and with rising grounds on each outside of the meadows, those grounds, having some hop-gardens and some pretty woods. But, though I was born in this vale, I must confess, that the ten miles between Maidstone and Tunbridge (which the Kentish folks call the *Garden of Eden*) is a great deal finer; for here, with a river three times as big and a vale three times as broad, there are, on rising grounds six times as broad, not only hop-gardens and beautiful woods, but immense orchards of apples, pears, plums, cherries and filberts, and these, in many cases, with gooseberries and currants and raspberries beneath; and, all taken together, the vale is really worthy of the appellation which it bears. But, even this spot, which I believe to be the very finest, as to fertility and diminutive beauty, in this whole world, I, for my part, do not like so well; nay, as a spot to *live on*, I think nothing at all of it, compared with a country where high downs prevail, with here and there a large wood on the top or the side of a hill, and where you see, in the deep dells, here and there a farm-house, and here and there a village, the buildings sheltered by a group of lofty trees.

This is my taste, and here, in the north of Hampshire, it has its full gratification. I like to look at the winding side of a great down, with two or three numerous flocks of sheep on it, belonging to different farms; and to see, lower down, the folds, in the fields, ready to receive them for the night. We had, when we got upon the downs, after leaving Winchester, this sort of country all the way to Whitchurch. Our point of destination was this village of Burghclere, which lies close under the north side of the lofty hill at HIGHCLERE, which is called Beacon-hill, and on the top of which there are still the marks of a Roman encampment. We saw this hill as soon as we got on Winchester downs; and without any regard to *roads*, we *steered* for it, as sailors do for a land-mark. Of these 13 miles (from Winchester to Whitchurch) we rode about eight or nine upon the *greensward*, or over fields equally smooth. And, here is one great pleasure of living in countries of this sort: no sloughs, no ditches, no nasty dirty lanes, and the hedges, where there are any, are more for boundary marks than for fences. Fine for hunting and coursing: no impediments; no gates to open; nothing to impede the dogs, the horses, or the view. The water is not *seen running*; but the great bed of chalk *holds it*, and the sun draws it up for the benefit of the grass and the corn; and, whatever inconvenience is experienced from the necessity of *deep wells*, and of driving sheep and cattle far to water, is amply made up for by the *goodness of the water*, and by the complete absence of floods, of drains, of ditches and of water-furrows. As *things now are*, however, these countries have one great draw-back: the poor day-labourers suffer from the want of fuel, and they have nothing but their *bare pay*. For these reasons they are greatly worse off than those of the *woodland countries*; and it is really surprising what a difference there is between the faces that you see here, and the round, red faces that you see in the *wealds* and the *forests*, particularly in *Sussex*, where the labourers *will* have a *meat-pudding* of some sort or other; and where they *will* have a *fire* to sit by in the winter.

After steering for some time, we came down to a very fine farm-house, which we stopped a little to admire; and I asked Richard whether *that* was not a place to be happy in. The village, which we found to be STOKE-CHARITY, was about a mile lower down this little vale. Before we got to it, we overtook the owner of the farm, who knew me, though I did not know him; but, when I found it was Mr HINTON BAILEY, of whom and whose farm I had heard so much, I was not at all surprised at the fineness of what I had just seen. I told him that the word *charity*, making, as it did, part of the name of this place, had nearly inspired me with boldness enough to go to the farm house, in the ancient style, and ask for something to eat; for, that we had not yet breakfasted. He asked us to go back; but, at BURGHCLERE we were *resolved to dine*. After, however, crossing the village, and beginning again to ascend the downs, we came to a labourer's (*once a farm house*), where I asked the man, whether he had any *bread and cheese*, and was not a little pleased to hear him say '*Yes*'. Then I asked him to give us a bit, protesting that we had not yet broken our fast. He answered in the affirmative, at once, though I did not talk of payment. His wife brought out the cut loaf, and a piece of Wiltshire cheese, and I took them in hand, gave Richard a good hunch, and took another for myself. I verily believe, that all the pleasure of eating enjoyed by all the feeders in London in a whole year, does not equal that which we enjoyed in gnawing this bread and cheese, as we rode over this cold down, whip and bridle-reins in one hand, and the hunch in the other. Richard, who was purse bearer, gave the woman, by my direction, about enough to buy two quartern loaves: for she told me, that they had to buy their bread *at the mill*, not being able to bake themselves for *want of fuel*; and this, as I said before, is one of the draw-backs in this sort of country. I wish every one of these people had an *American fire-place*. Here they might, then, even in these bare countries have comfortable warmth. Rubbish of any sort would, by this means, give them warmth. I am now, at six o'clock in the morning, sitting in a room, where one of these fire-places, with very light *turf* in it, gives as good and steady a warmth as it is possible to feel, and which room has, too, been *cured of smoking* by this fire-place.

Before we got this supply of bread and cheese, we, though in ordinary times a couple of singularly jovial companions, and seldom going a hundred yards (except going very fast) without one or the other speaking, began to grow *dull*, or rather *glum*. The way seemed long; and, when I had to speak in answer to Richard, the speaking was as brief as might be. Unfortunately, just at this critical period, one of the loops that held the straps of Richard's little portmanteau broke; and it became necessary (just before we overtook Mr Bailey) for me to fasten the portmanteau on before me, upon my saddle. This, which was not the work of more than five minutes, would, had I had *a breakfast*, have been nothing at all, and, indeed, matter of laughter. But, *now*, it was *something*. It was his *'fault'* for capering and jerking about *'so'*. I jumped off, saying, *'Here!* I'll carry it *myself.'* And then I began to take off the remaining strap, pulling, with great violence and in great haste. Just at this time, my eyes met his, in which I saw *great surprise*; and, feeling the just rebuke, feeling heartily ashamed of myself, I instantly changed my tone and manner, cast the blame upon the saddler, and talked of the effectual means which we would take to prevent the like in future.

Now, if such was the effect produced upon me by the want of food for only two or three hours; me, who had dined well the day before and eaten toast and butter the over-night; if the missing of only one breakfast, and that, too, from my own whim, while I had money in my pocket, to get one at any public-house, and while I could get one only for asking for at any farm-house; if the not having breakfasted could, and under such circumstances, make me what you may call *'cross'* to a child like this, whom I must necessarily love so much, and to whom I never speak but in the very kindest manner; if this mere absence of a breakfast could thus put me *out of temper*, how great are the allowances that we ought to make for the poor creatures, who, in this once happy and now miserable country, are doomed to lead a life of constant labour and of half-starvation. I suppose, that, as we rode away from the cottage, we gnawed up, between us, a pound of bread and a quarter of a pound of cheese. Here was about *five-pence* worth at present prices. Even this, which was only a mere *snap*, a mere *stay-stomach*, for us, would, for us two, come to 3*s*. a week all but a penny. How, then, gracious God! is a labouring man, his wife, and, perhaps, four or five small children, to exist upon 8*s*. or 9*s*. a week! Aye, and to find house-rent, clothing, bedding and fuel out of it? Richard and I ate here, at this snap, more, and much more, than the average of labourers, their wives and children, have to eat in a whole day, and that the labourer has to *work* on too!

When we got here to Burghclere, we were again as *hungry* as hunters. What, then, must be the life of these poor creatures? But is not the state of the country, is not the hellishness of the system, all depicted in this one disgraceful and damning fact, that the magistrates, who settle on what the *labouring poor* ought to have to live on, ALLOW THEM LESS THAN IS ALLOWED TO FELONS IN THE GAOLS, and allow them *nothing for clothing and fuel, and house-rent!* And yet, while this is notoriously the case, while the main body of the working class in England are fed and clad and even lodged worse than felons, and are daily becoming even worse and worse off, the King is advised to tell the Parliament, and the world, that we are in a state of *unexampled prosperity*, and that this prosperity must be *permanent*, because *all the* GREAT *interests are prospering!* The working people are not, then, 'a *great* interest'! They will be found to be one, by-and-by. What is to be the *end* of this? What can be the end of it, but dreadful convulsion? What other can be produced by a system, which allows the *felon* better food, better clothing, and better lodging than the *honest labourer?*

I see that there has been a grand *humanity-meeting* in Norfolk, to assure the parliament, that these humanity-people will *back* it in any measures that it may adopt for freeing the NEGROES. Mr BUXTON figured here, also LORD SUFFIELD, who appear to have been the two principal actors, or *showers-off*. This same Mr BUXTON opposed the bill intended to relieve the *poor in England* by breaking a little into the *brewers' monopoly*; and, as to Lord Suffield, if he really wish to free slaves, let him go to Wykham in this county, where he will see some *drawing, like horses*, gravel to repair the roads for the *stock-jobbers* and *dead-weight* and the *seat-dealers* to ride smoothly on. If he go down a little further, he will see CONVICTS at PRECISELY THE SAME WORK, harnessed in JUST THE SAME WAY; but, the convicts he will find hale and ruddy-cheeked, in dresses sufficiently warm, and bawling and singing; while he will find the labourers thin, ragged, shivering, dejected mortals, such as never were seen in any other country upon earth. There is not a negro in the West-Indies, who has not more to eat *in a day*, than the average of English labourers have to eat *in a week*, and of better food too. COLONEL WODEHOUSE and a man of the name of HOSEASON, (whence came he?) who opposed this humanity-scheme, talked of *the sums necessary to pay the owners of the slaves*. They took special care not to tell the humanity-men *to look at home for slaves to free*. No, no! that would have applied to themselves, as well as to Lord SUFFIELD and humanity BUXTON. If it were worth while to *reason* with these people, one might ask them, whether they do not think, that *another war* is likely to relieve them of all these cares, simply by making the colonies transfer their allegiance, or assert their independence? But, to reason with them is useless. If they can busy themselves with compassion for the negroes, while they uphold the system that makes the labourers of England more wretched, and beyond all measure more wretched, than any negro slaves are, or ever were, or ever can be, they are unworthy of any thing but our contempt.

But, the 'education' canters are the most curious fellows of all. They have seen 'education', as they call it, and *crimes*, go on *increasing together*, till the gaols, though of six times their former dimensions, will hardly suffice; and yet, the canting creatures still cry, that crimes arise from want of what they call '*education*'! They see the FELON *better fed and better clad* than the HONEST LABOURER. They see this; and yet they continually cry, that the crimes arise from a want of '*education*'! What can be the cause of this perverseness? It is not perverseness: it is *roguery*, *corruption*, and *tyranny*. The tyrant, the unfeeling tyrant, squeezes the labourers for gain's sake; and the corrupt politician and literary or tub rogue, find an excuse for him by pretending, that it is *not want of food and clothing*, but *want of education*, that makes the poor, starving wretches thieves and robbers. If the press, if only the press, were to do its duty, or but a tenth part of its duty, this hellish system could not go on. But, it favours the system by ascribing the misery to wrong causes. The causes are these: the tax-gatherer presses the landlord; the landlord the farmer; and the farmer the labourer. Here it falls at last; and this class is made so miserable, that a *felon's* life is better than that of a *labourer*. Does there want any *other cause* to produce crimes? But, on these causes, so clear to the eye of reason, so plain from experience, the press scarcely ever says a single word; while it keeps bothering our brains about *education* and *morality*; and about ignorance and immorality leading to *felonies*. To be sure immorality leads to felonies. Who does not know that? But, who is to expect *morality* in a *half-starved man*, who is *whipped if he do not work*, though he has not, for his whole day's food, so much as I and my little boy snapped up in six or seven minutes upon Stoke-Charity down? Aye! but, if the press were to ascribe the increase of crimes to the true causes, it must *go further back*. It must go to the *cause of the taxes*. It must go to the debt, the dead-weight, the thundering standing army, the enormous sinecures, pensions, and grants; and this would suit but a very small part of *a press*, which lives and thrives principally by one or the other of these.

As with the press, so is it with Mr BROUGHAM, and all such politicians. They stop short, or, rather, they begin in the middle. They attempt to prevent the evils of the deadly ivy by cropping off, or, rather, bruising a little, a few of its leaves. They do not assail even its branches, while they appear to look upon the *trunk* as something *too sacred* even to be *looked at* with vulgar eyes. Is not the injury recently done to about *forty thousand poor*

families in and near Plymouth, by the Small-note Bill, a
thing that Mr Brougham ought to think about before
he thinks any thing more about *educating* those poor
families? Yet, will he, when he again meets the Ministers,
say a word about this monstrous evil? I am afraid that
no Member will say a word about it; but, I am rather
more than afraid, that *he* will not. And, *why?* Because, if
he reproach the Ministers with this crying cruelty, they
will ask him first, how this is to be prevented without a
repeal of the Small-note Bill (by which Peel's Bill was
partly repealed); then they will ask him, how the prices
are to be kept up without the small-notes; then they will
say, 'Does the honourable and learned Gentleman *wish
to see wheat at four shillings a bushel again?'*

B. No, (looking at Mr WESTERN and DADDY COKE)
no, no, no! Upon my honour, no!

MIN. Does the honourable and learned Gentleman
wish to see Cobbett again at county meetings, and to
see petitions again coming from those meetings, calling
for a reduction of the interest of the . . . ?

B. No, no, no! upon my soul, no!

MIN. Does the honourable and learned Gentleman
wish to see that *equitable* adjustment, which Cobbett has
a thousand times declared can never take place without
an application, to new purposes, *of that great mass of
public property, commonly called Church property?*

B. (Almost bursting with rage) How *dare* the honourable gentlemen to suppose me capable of such a thought?

MIN. We suppose nothing. We only ask the question;
and we ask it, because to put an end to the small-notes
would inevitably produce all these things; and, it is

impossible to have small-notes to the extent necessary to *keep up prices*, without having, now-and-then, *breaking banks*. Banks cannot break without *producing misery*; you must have the *consequence*, if you will have the *cause*. The honourable and learned Gentleman wants the feast without the reckoning. In short, is the honourable and learned Gentleman for putting an end to '*public credit*'?

B. No, no, no, no!

MIN. Then would it not be better for the honourable and learned Gentleman to *hold his tongue?*

All men of sense and sincerity will, at once, answer this last question in the affirmative. They will all say, that this is not *opposition* to the Ministers. The Ministers do not *wish* to see 40,000 families, nor any families at all (who give them *no real annoyance*), reduced to misery; they do not *wish* to cripple their own tax-payers; very far from it. If they could carry on the debt and dead-weight and place and pension and barrack system, without reducing any *quiet* people to misery, they would like it exceedingly. But, they *do wish to carry on that system*; and he does not *oppose* them who does not endeavour to put an end to the system. This is done by nobody in Parliament; and, therefore, there is, in fact, *no opposition*; and this is felt by the whole nation; and this is the reason why *the people* now take so little interest in what is said and done in Parliament, compared to that which they formerly took. This is the reason why there is no man, or men, whom the people seem to care at all about. A great portion of the people now clearly understand the nature and effects of the system; they are not now to be deceived by speeches and professions. If PITT and FOX had *now to start*, there would be no 'PITTITES' and 'FOXITES'. Those happy days of political humbug are gone for ever. The 'gentlemen *opposite*' are opposite only as to mere *local position*. They sit on the opposite side of the house: that's all. In every other respect they are like parson and clerk; or, perhaps, rather more like the rooks and jack-daws: one *caw* and the other *chatter*; but both have the same object in view: both are in pursuit of the same sort of diet. One set is, to be sure, IN place, and the other OUT; but, though the rooks keep the jack-daws on the inferior branches, these latter would be as clamorous as the rooks themselves against FELLING THE TREE; and just as clamorous would the 'gentlemen opposite' be against any one who should propose to put down the system itself. And yet, unless you do *that*, things must go on in the present way, and FELONS must be BETTER FED than HONEST LABOURERS; and starvation and thieving and robbing and gaol-building and transporting and hanging and penal laws must go on increasing, as they have gone on from the day of the establishment of the debt to the present hour. Apropos of *penal laws*. Doctor Black (of the Morning Chronicle) is now filling whole columns with very just remarks on the new and terrible law, which makes the taking of an apple FELONY; but, he says not a word about the *silence* of SIR JAMMY (the humane *code-softener*) upon this subject! The '*humanity and liberality*' of the Parliament have relieved men addicted to *fraud* and to *unnatural crimes* from the disgrace of the pillory, and they have, since CASTLEREAGH cut his own throat, relieved *self-slayers* from the disgrace of the cross-road burial; but the same Parliament, amidst all the workings of this rare *humanity* and *liberality*, have made it *felony to take an apple off a tree*, which last year was a trivial trespass, and was formerly no offence at all! However, even this *is necessary*, as long as this bank note system continue in its present way; and all complaints about severity of laws, levelled at the poor, are useless and foolish; and these complaints are even base in those who do their best to uphold a system, which has brought *the honest labourer to be fed worse than the felon*. What, *short of such laws*, can prevent *starving men* from coming to take away the dinners of those who have plenty? '*Education*'! Despicable cant and nonsense! What education, what moral precepts, can quiet the gnawings and ragings of hunger?

Looking, now, back again, for a minute, to the little village of *Stoke-Charity*, the name of which seems to indicate, that its rents formerly belonged wholly to the poor and indigent part of the community. It is near to Winchester, that grand scene of ancient learning, piety and munificence. Be this as it may, the parish formerly contained *ten farms*, and it now contains but *two*, which are owned by Mr *Hinton Bailey* and *his nephew*, and, therefore, which may probably become *one*. There used to be *ten well-fed families* in this parish, at any rate: these, taking *five* to a family, made *fifty* well-fed people. And, now, all are half-starved, except the *curate* and the two families. The *blame* is not the landowner's; it is nobody's; it is due to the infernal *funding* and *taxing* system, which *of necessity* drives property into large masses in order to *save itself*; which crushes little proprietors down into labourers; and which presses them down in that state, there takes their wages from them and makes them *paupers*, their share of food and raiment being taken away to support debt and dead-weight and army and all the rest of the enormous expenses, which are required to sustain this intolerable system. Those, therefore, are fools or hypocrites, who affect to wish to better the lot of the poor labourers and manufacturers, while they, at the same time, either actively or passively, uphold the system which is the manifest cause of it. Here is a system, which, clearly as the nose upon your face, you see taking away the little gentleman's estate, the little farmer's farm, the poor labourer's meat-dinner and Sunday-coat; and, while you see this so plainly, you, fool or hypocrite, as you are, cry out for supporting the system that causes it all! Go on, base wretch; but, remember, that of such a progress dreadful must be the end. The day will come, when millions of long-suffering creatures will be in a state that they and you now little dream of. All that we now behold of *combinations*, and the like, are mere *indications* of what the great body of the suffering people *feel*, and of the thoughts that are passing in their minds. The *coaxing* work of *schools* and *tracts* will only add to what would be quite enough without them. There is not a labourer in the whole country, who does not see to the bottom of this *coaxing* work. They are *not deceived* in this respect. Hunger has opened their eyes. I'll engage that there is not, even in this obscure village of *Stoke-Charity*, one single creature, however forlorn, who does not understand all about the *real motives* of the school and the tract and the Bible affair as well as Butterworth, or Rivington, or as Joshua Watson himself.

Just after we had finished the bread and cheese, we crossed the turnpike road that goes from Basingstoke to Stockbridge; and Mr Bailey had told us, that we were then to bear away to our right, and go to the end of a wood (which we saw one end of), and keep round with that wood, or *coppice*, as he called it, to our left; but we, seeing *Beacon-Hill* more to the left, and resolving to go, as nearly as possible, in a straight line to it, steered directly over the fields; that is to say, pieces of ground from 30 to 100 acres in each. But, a hill, which we had to go over, had here hidden from our sight a part of this '*coppice*', which consists, perhaps, of 150 or 200 acres, and which we found sweeping round, in a crescent-like form so far, from towards our left, as to bring our *land-mark* over the coppice at about the mid-length of the latter. Upon this discovery we slackened sail; for this coppice might be a mile across; and though the bottom was sound enough, being a coverlet of flints upon a bed of chalk, the underwood was too high and too thick for us to face, being, as we were, at so great a distance from the means of obtaining a fresh supply of clothes. Our leather leggings would have stood any thing; but, our coats were of the common kind; and, before we saw the other side of the coppice we should, I dare say, have been as ragged as forest-ponies in the month of March.

In this dilemma I stopped and looked at the coppice. Luckily two boys, who had been cutting sticks (*to sell*, I dare say, at least *I hope so*), made their appearance, at about half a mile off, on the side for the coppice. Richard galloped off to the boys, from whom he found, that, in one part of the coppice, there was a road cut across, the point of entrance into which road they explained to him. This was to us, what the discovery of a canal across the isthmus of Darien would be to a ship in the Gulph of Mexico, wanting to get into the Pacific without doubling Cape-Horne. A beautiful road we found it. I should suppose the best part of a mile long, *perfectly straight*, the surface sound and smooth, about *eight feet* wide, the whole length seen at once, and, when you are at one end, the other end seeming to be hardly a yard wide. When we got about half way, we found a road that crossed this. These roads are, I suppose, cut for the hunters. They are very pretty, at any rate, and we found this one very convenient; for it cut our way short by a full half mile.

From this coppice, to Whitchurch, is not more than about four miles, and we soon reached it, because here you begin to descend into the *vale*, in which this little town lies, and through which there runs that *stream*, which turns the mill of 'SQUIRE PORTAL, and which mill makes the *Bank of England Note-Paper!* Talk of the THAMES and the HUDSON, with their forests of masts; talk of the NILE and the DELAWARE, bearing the food of millions on their bosoms; talk of the Ganges and the Mississippi sending forth over the world their silks and their cottons; talk of the Rio de la Plata and the other rivers, their beds pebbled with silver and gold and dia-monds. What, as to their effect on the condition of mankind, as to the virtues, the vices, the enjoyments and the sufferings of men; what are all these rivers put together, compared with the *river of Whitchurch*, which a man of threescore may jump across dry-shod, which moistens a quarter of a mile wide of poor, rushy meadow, which washes the skirts of the park and game-preserves of that bright patrician, who wedded the daughter of HANSON, the attorney and late solicitor to the Stamp-Office, and which is, to look at it, of far less importance than any gutter in the WEN! Yet, this river, by merely turning a wheel, which wheel sets some rag-tearers and grinders and washers and recompressers in motion, has produced a greater effect on the condition of men, than has been produced on that condition by all the other rivers, all the seas, all the mines and all the continents in the world. The discovery of America, and the consequent discovery and use of vast quantities of silver and gold, did, indeed, produce great effects on the nations of Europe. They changed the value of money, and caused, as all such changes must, a *transfer of property*, raising up new families and pulling down old ones, a transfer very little favourable either to *morality*, or to real and *substantial liberty*. But this cause worked *slowly*; its consequences came on by slow *degrees*; it made a transfer of property, but it made that transfer in so small a degree, and it left the property quiet in the hands of the new possessor *for so long a time*, that the effect was not violent, and was not, at any rate, such as to uproot possessors by whole districts, as the hurricane uproots the forests.

Not so the product of the little sedgy rivulet of Whitchurch! It has, in the short space of *a hundred and thirty-one years*, and, indeed, in the space of the last FORTY, caused greater changes as to property than had been caused by all other things put together in the long course of seven centuries, though, during that course there had been a sweeping, confiscating Protestant reformation. Let us look back to the place where I started, on this present rural ride. Poor old BARON MASERES, succeeded, at REIGATE, by little PARSON FELLOWES, and at BETCH-WORTH (three miles on my road) by KENDRICK, is no bad instance to begin with; for, the Baron was nobly descended, though from French ancestors. At ALDBURY, fifteen miles on my road, Mr DRUMMOND (a banker) is in the seat of one of the HOWARDS, and, close by, he has bought the estate, just pulled down the house, and blotted out the memory of the GODSCHALLS. At CHIL-WORTH, two miles further down the same vale, and close under St MARTHA's HILL, Mr TINKLER, a powder-maker (succeeding HILL, another powder-maker, who had been a *breeches-maker* at Hounslow) has got the old mansion and the estate of the old DUCHESS of MARLBOROUGH, who frequently resided in what was then a large quad-rangular mansion, but the remains of which now serve as out farm-buildings and a farm-house, which I found inhabited by *a poor labourer and his family*, the farm being in the hands of the powder-maker, who does not find the once noble seat good enough for him. Coming on to WAVERLEY ABBEY, there is Mr THOMPSON, a merchant, succeeding the ORBY HUNTERS and Sir ROBERT RICH. Close adjoining, Mr LAING, a *West India dealer of some sort*, has stepped into the place of the lineal descendants of Sir WILLIAM TEMPLE. At FARNHAM the park and palace remain in the hands of a Bishop of Winchester, as they have done for about *eight hundred years*; but *why* is this? Because they are *public property*; because they *cannot*, without express laws, be transferred.

Therefore the product of the rivulet of Whitchurch has had no effect upon the ownership of these, which are still in the hands of *a Bishop of Winchester*; not of a *William of Wykham*, to be sure; but still, in those of *a bishop*, at any rate. Coming on to OLD ALRESFORD (twenty miles from Farnham) SHERIFF, the son of a SHERIFF, who was a *Commissary in the American war*, has succeeded the GAGES. Two miles further on, at ABBOTSTON (down on the side of the Itchen) ALEXANDER BARING has succeeded the heirs and successors of the DUKE OF BOLTON, the remains of whose noble mansion I once saw here. Not above a mile higher up, the same Baring has, at the GRANGE, with its noble mansion, park and estate, succeeded the heirs of LORD NORTHINGTON; and, at only about two miles further, Sir THOMAS BARING, at Stratton Park, has succeeded the RUSSELLS in the ownership of the estates of Stratton and Micheldever, which were once the property of ALFRED THE GREAT! Stepping back, and following my road, down by the side of the meadows of the beautiful river Itchen, and coming to Easton, I look across to MARTYR'S WORTHY, and there see (as I observed before) the OGLES succeeded by a *general* or a *colonel, somebody*; but who, or whence, I cannot learn.

This is all in less than four score miles, from Reigate even to this place, where I now am. Oh! mighty rivulet of Whitchurch! All our properties, all our laws, all our manners, all our minds, you have changed! This, which I have noticed, has all taken place within forty, and, most of it, within *ten* years. The *small gentry*, to about the *third* rank upwards (considering there to be five ranks from the smallest gentry up to the greatest nobility,) are *all gone*, nearly to a man, and the small farmers along with them. The Barings alone have, I should think, swallowed up thirty or forty of these small gentry without perceiving it. They, indeed, swallow up the biggest race of all; but, innumerable small fry slip down unperceived, like caplins down the throats of the sharks, while these latter *feel* only the cod-fish. It frequently happens, too, that a big gentleman or nobleman, whose estate has been big enough to resist for a long while, and who has swilled up many caplin-gentry, goes down the throat of the loan-dealer with all the caplins in his belly.

Thus the Whitchurch rivulet goes on, shifting property from hand to hand. The big, in order to save themselves from being '*swallowed up quick*' (as we used to be taught to say, in our Church Prayers against Buonaparte,) make use of their *voices* to get, through place, pension, or sinecure, something back from the taxers. Others of them *fall in love* with the *daughters* and *widows* of paper-money people, big brewers, and the like; and sometimes their daughters *fall in love* with the paper-money people's sons, or the fathers of those sons; and, whether they be *Jews*, or not, seems to be little matter with this all-subduing passion of love. But, the *small gentry* have no resource. While *war* lasted, '*glorious* war', there was a resource; but *now*, alas! not only is there no war, but there is *no hope of war*; and, not a few of them will actually come to the *parish-book*. There is no place for them in the army, church, navy, customs, excise, pension-list, or any where else. All these are now wanted by 'their *betters*'. A stock-jobber's family will not look at such pennyless things. So that while they have been the active, the zealous, the efficient instruments, in compelling the working classes to submit to half-starvation, they have, at any rate been brought to the most abject ruin themselves; *for which I most heartily thank God.* The 'harvest of war' is never to return without a total blowing up of the paper-system. Spain must belong to France, St Domingo must pay her tribute. *America must be paid for slaves taken away in war,* she must have Florida, she must go on openly and avowedly making a navy for the purpose of humbling us; and all this, and ten times more, if France and America should choose; and yet, we can have *no war,* as long as the paper-system last; and, if *that cease,* then *what is to come!*

Burghclere,
Sunday Morning, 6th November

It has been fine all the week, until to-day, when we intended to set off for HURSTBOURN-TARRANT, vulgarly called UPHUSBAND, but the *rain* seems as if it would stop us. From Whitchurch to within two miles of this place, it is the same sort of country as between Winchester and Whitchurch. High, chalk bottom, open downs or large fields, with here and there a *farm-house in a dell,* sheltered by lofty trees, which, to my taste, is the most pleasant situation in the world.

This has been with Richard, *one whole week* of hare-hunting, and with me, three days and a half. The weather has been amongst the finest that I ever saw, and Lord Caernarvon's preserves fill the country with hares, while these hares invite us to ride about and to see his park and estate, at this fine season of the year, in every direction. We are now on the north side of that Beacon-hill for which we steered last Sunday. This makes part of a chain of lofty chalk-hills and downs, which divides all the lower part of Hampshire from Berkshire, though, the ancient ruler, owner, of the former, took a little strip all along, on the flat, on this side of the chain, in order I suppose, to make the ownership of the hills themselves the more clear of all dispute; just as the owner of a field hedge and bank owns also the ditch on his neighbour's side. From these hills you look, at one view, over the whole of Berkshire, into Oxfordshire, Gloucestershire and Wiltshire, and you can see the Isle of Wight and the sea. On this north side the chalk soon ceases, the sand and clay begin, and the oak-woods cover a great part of the surface. Amongst these is the farm-house, in which we are, and from the warmth and good fare of which we do not mean to stir, until we can do it without the chance of a wet skin.

This rain has given me time to look at the newspapers of *about a week old*. Oh, oh! The *Cotton Lords* are *tearing!* Thank God for that! The *Lords of the Anvil are snapping!* Thank God for that too! They have kept poor souls, then, in a heat of 84 degrees to little purpose, after all. The *'great interests'* mentioned in the King's Speech, do not, *then*, all continue to flourish! The 'prosperity' was not, then, *'permanent'* though the King was advised to assert so positively that it was! 'Anglo-Mexican and Pasco-Peruvian' fall in price, and the Chronicle assures me, that the *'respectable* owners of the *Mexican Mining* shares mean to take measures to protect their *property*'. Indeed! Like *protecting* the Spanish Bonds, I suppose? Will the Chronicle be so good as to tell us the names of these '*respectable* persons'? Doctor Black must *know* their *names*; or else he could not know them to be *respectable*. If the parties be those that I have heard, these mining works may possibly operate with them as an *emetic*, and make them *throw-up* a part, at least, of what they have taken down.

There has, I see, at *New York*, been that confusion, which I, four months ago, said would and must take place; that breaking of merchants and all the ruin, which, in such a case, spreads itself about, ruining families and producing fraud and despair. Here will be, between the two countries, an interchange of cause and effect, proceeding from the dealings in *cotton*, until, first and last, two or three hundred thousands of persons have, at one spell of paper-money work, been made to drink deep of misery. I pity none but the poor English creatures, who are compelled to work on the wool of this accursed weed, which has done so much mischief to England. The slaves who cultivate and gather the cotton, are *well fed*. They do not suffer. The sufferers are those who spin it and weave it and colour it, and the wretched beings who cover with it those bodies, which, as in the time of Old FORTESCUE, ought to be '*clothed throughout in good woollens*'.

One newspaper says, that Mr HUSKISSON is gone to Paris, and thinks it *likely* that he will endeavour to 'inculcate in *the mind of the Bourbons wise principles of free trade*'! What the devil next! Persuade them, I suppose, that it is for *their good*, that English goods should be admitted into France and into St Domingo, with little or no duty? Persuade them to make a treaty of commerce with him; and, in short, persuade them to make *France help to pay the interest of our debt and dead-weight*, lest our system of paper should go to pieces, and lest that should be followed by *a radical reform*, which reform would be injurious to 'the *monarchical principle*'! This newspaper politician does, however, *think*, that the Bourbons will be '*too dull*' to comprehend these '*enlightened* and *liberal*' notions; and I think so too. I think the Bourbons, or, rather, those who will speak for them, will say: 'No thank you. You contracted your *debt* without our participation; you made your *dead-weight* for your own purposes; the seizure of our museums and the loss of our frontier towns followed your victory of Waterloo, though we were "your ALLIES" at the time; you made us pay an enormous TRIBUTE after that battle, and kept possession of part of France till we had paid it; you *wished*, the other day, to keep us out of Spain, and you, Mr HUSKISSON, in a speech at Liverpool, called our deliverance of the King of Spain an *unjust and unprincipled act of aggression*, while Mr Canning *prayed to God* that we might not succeed. No thank you, Mr HUSKISSON, no. No coaxing, Sir; we saw, then, too clearly the *advantage we derived from your having a debt and a dead-weight*, to wish to assist in relieving you from either. "*Monarchical principle*" here, or "*monarchical principle*" there, we know, that your mill-stone debt is our best security. We like to have your *wishes*, your *prayers*, and your *abuse* against us, rather than your *subsidies* and your *fleets:* and so, farewell, Mr

HUSKISSON: if you like, the English may drink French wine; but whether they do or not, the French shall not wear your rotten cottons. And, as a last word, how did you maintain the *"monarchical principle"* the *"paternal principle"* or as CASTLEREAGH called it, the *"social system"*, when you called that an unjust and unprincipled aggression, which put an end to the bargain, by which the convents and other church-property of Spain were to be transferred to the Jews and Jobbers of London? Bon jour, Monsieur Huskisson, ci-devant membre et orateur du club de quatre vingt neuf !'

If they do not actually *say* this to him, this is what they will *think*; and that is, as to the effect, precisely the same thing. It is childishness to suppose, that any nation will act from a desire of *serving all other nations, or any one other nation, as well as itself.* It will make, unless compelled, no compact, by which it does not think itself *a gainer*; and, amongst its gains, it must, and always does, reckon the injury to its rivals. It is a stupid idea, that *all nations are to gain*, by any thing. Whatever is the gain of one, must, in some way or other, be a loss to another. So that this new project of *'free trade'* and *'mutual gain'* is as pure a humbug as that which the newspapers carried on, during the *'glorious days'* of *loans*, when they told us, at every loan, that the bargain was *'equally advantageous* to the *contractors* and to *the public'!* The fact is, the 'free trade' project is clearly the effect of a *consciousness of our weakness.* As long as we felt *strong*, we felt *bold*, we had no thought of *conciliating* the world; we upheld a system of *exclusion*, which long experience proved to be founded in *sound policy.* But, we now find, that our debts and our loads of various sorts cripple us. We feel our incapacity for the *carrying of trade sword in hand:* and so, we have given up all our old maxims, and are endeavouring to persuade the world, that we are anxious to enjoy no advantages that are not enjoyed also by our neighbours. Alas! the world *sees very clearly* the cause of all this; and the world *laughs at us* for our imaginary cunning. My old doggrel, that used to make me and my friends laugh in Long-Island is precisely pat to this case.

> When his maw was stuff 'd with paper,
> How JOHN BULL did prance and caper!
> How he foam'd and how he roar'd:
> How his neighbours all he gored!
> How he scrap'd the ground and hurl'd
> Dirt and filth on all the world!
> But JOHN BULL of paper empty,
> Though in midst of peace and plenty,
> Is modest grown as worn-out sinner,
> As Scottish laird that wants a dinner;
> As WILBERFORCE, become content
> A rotten burgh to represent;
> As BLUE and BUFF, when, after hunting
> On Yankee coasts their *'bits of bunting'*,
> Came softly back across the seas,
> And silent were as mice in cheese.

Yes, the whole world, and particularly the French and the Yankees, see very clearly the *course* of this fit of *modesty* and of *liberality*, into which we have so recently fallen. They know well, that a *war* would play the very devil with our *national faith*. They know, in short, that no Ministers in their senses will think of supporting the paper system through another war. They know well, that no ministers that now exist, or are likely to exist, will venture to endanger the paper-system; and therefore they know that (for England) they may now do just what they please. When the French were about to invade Spain, Mr CANNING said that his last dispatch on the subject was to be understood as a *protest*, on the part of England, *against permanent occupation* of any part of Spain by France. *There the French are*, however; and at the end of *two years and a half*, he says that he *knows nothing about* any intention that they have to quit Spain, or any part of it!

Why, Saint Domingo *was* independent. We had traded with it as an *independent state*. Is it not clear, that if we had *said the word*, (and had been known to be able to *arm*), France would not have attempted to treat that fine and rich country as a colony? Mark how wise this measure of France! How *just*, too; to obtain, by means of a *tribute* from the St Domingoians, compensation for the *loyalists* of that country! Was this done with regard to the *loyalists of America*, in the reign of the good jubilee George III? Oh, no! Those loyalists had to be paid, and many of them have *even yet*, at the end of more than *half a century*, to be paid out of taxes raised *on us*, for the losses occasioned by their *disinterested loyalty!* This was a master-stroke on the part of France; she gets about seven millions sterling in the way of tribute; she makes that rich island yield to her great commercial advantages; and she, at the same time, paves the way for effecting one of two objects; namely, getting the island back again, or throwing our islands into confusion, whenever it shall be her interest to do it.

This might have been prevented by a *word* from us, if we had *been ready for war*. But we are grown *modest*; we are grown *liberal*; we do not want to engross that which fairly belongs to our neighbours! We have undergone a change, somewhat like that which marriage produces on a blustering fellow, who, while single, can but just clear his teeth. This change is quite surprising, and especially by the time that the second child comes, the man is *loaded*; he looks like a loaded man; his voice becomes so soft and gentle compared to what it used to be. Just such are the effects of *our load:* but the worst of it is, our neighbours are *not thus loaded*. However, far be it from me to *regret* this, or any part of it. The *load* is *the people's best friend*. If that could, *without reform*; if that could be shaken off, leaving the *seat-men* and the *parsons* in their present state, *I would not live in England another day!* And I say this with as much seriousness as if I were upon my death-bed.

The wise men of the newspapers are for a repeal of the *Corn Laws*. With all my heart, I will join any body in a petition for their repeal. But, *this will not be done*. We shall stop short of this extent of '*liberality*', let what may be the consequence to the manufacturers. The Cotton Lords must all go, to the last man, rather than a repeal, these laws will take place: and of this the newspaper wise men may be assured. The farmers can but *just rub along now*, with all their high prices and low wages. What would be their state, and that of their landlords, if the wheat were to come down again 4, 5, or even 6 shillings a bushel? Universal agricultural bankruptcy would be the almost instant consequence. Many of them are now deep in debt from the effects of 1820, 1821, and 1822. One more year like 1822 would have broken the whole mass up, and left the lands to be cultivated, under the overseers, for the benefit of the paupers. Society would have been nearly dissolved, and the state of nature would have returned. The Small-Note Bill, *cooperating with the Corn Laws* have given a *respite*, and nothing more. This Bill must remain *efficient*, paper-money must cover the country, and the corn-laws must remain in force; OR, an 'equitable adjustment' must take place; OR, to a state of nature this country must return. What, then, as I want a repeal of the corn-laws, and also *want* to get rid of the paper-money *I must want to see this return to a state of nature?* By no means. I want the 'equitable adjustment', and I am quite sure, that no adjustment can be *equitable*, which does not apply *every penny's worth of public property* to the payment of the fund-holders and dead-weight and the like. Clearly *just* and *reasonable* as this is, however, the very mention of it makes the FIRE-SHOVELS, and some others, half mad. It makes them storm and rant and swear like Bedlamites. But it is curious to hear them talk of the *impracticability* of it; when they all know that, by only two or three acts of Parliament, Henry VIII did ten times as much as it would now, I hope, be necessary to do. If the duty were imposed *on me*, no statesman, legislator or lawyer, but a simple citizen, I think I could, in less than twenty-four hours, draw up an act, that would give satisfaction to, I will not say *every man*; but to, at least, ninety-nine out of every hundred; an act that would put all affairs of *money* and of *religion* to rights at once; but that would, I must confess, soon take from us that amiable *modesty*, of which I have spoken above, and which is so conspicuously shown in our works of *free-trade* and *liberality*.

The weather is clearing up; our horses are saddled, and we are off.

THE STORY OF PENGUIN CLASSICS

Before 1946 …'Classics' are mainly the domain of academics and students, without readable editions for everyone else. This all changes when a little-known classicist, E. V. Rieu, presents Penguin founder Allen Lane with the translation of Homer's *Odyssey* that he has been working on and reading to his wife Nelly in his spare time.

1946 The *Odyssey* becomes the first Penguin Classic published, and promptly sells three million copies. Suddenly, classic books are no longer for the privileged few.

1950s Rieu, now series editor, turns to professional writers for the best modern, readable translations, including Dorothy L. Sayers's *Inferno* and Robert Graves's *The Twelve Caesars*, which revives the salacious original.

1960s 1961 sees the arrival of the Penguin Modern Classics, showcasing the best twentieth-century writers from around the world. Rieu retires in 1964, hailing the Penguin Classics list as 'the greatest educative force of the 20th century'.

1970s A new generation of translators arrives to swell the Penguin Classics ranks, and the list grows to encompass more philosophy, religion, science, history and politics.

1980s The Penguin American Library joins the Classics stable, with titles such as *The Last of the Mohicans* safeguarded. Penguin Classics now offers the most comprehensive library of world literature available.

1990s Penguin Popular Classics are launched, offering readers budget editions of the greatest works of literature. Penguin Audiobooks brings the classics to a listening audience for the first time, and in 1999 the launch of the Penguin Classics website takes them online to an ever larger global readership.

The 21st Century Penguin Classics are rejacketed for the first time in nearly twenty years. This world famous series now consists of more than 1,300 titles, making the widest range of the best books ever written available to millions – and constantly redefining the meaning of what makes a 'classic'.

The *Odyssey* continues …

The best books ever written

PENGUIN (🐧) CLASSICS

SINCE 1946